THE AMAZING

WORLD BENEATH

THE WAVES

An Introduction to Understanding the Oceans

To the Greggs Family

Gloria Barnett

Illustrations by Tiki Graves

Gloria Barnett

With a foreword by John Aitchison
Wildlife Filmmaker

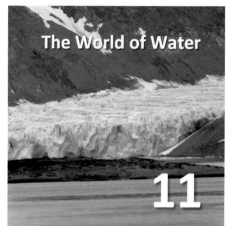

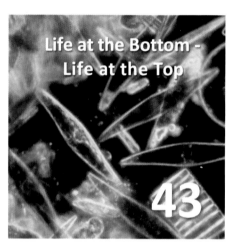

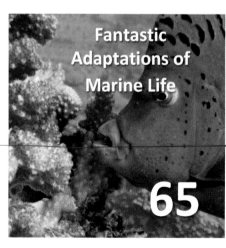

THE AMAZING

WORLD BENEATH

THE

WAVES

An Introduction to Understanding the
Oceans

Footprint to the Future Publishing

Front cover Photograph:
Green Sea Turtle Chelonia-mydas – Red Sea, Egypt
Photographer: Dray van Beeck
Back Cover Photograph
Coral Garden with Anemone Clownfish - Maldives
Photographer: Tiki Graves

First published - November 2011
Second edition - February 2014
THIRD EDITION – March 2021
ISBN: 978-1-8380643-7-2

The views expressed in this work are solely those of the author.

www.footprinttothefuture.co.uk

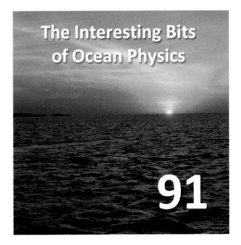
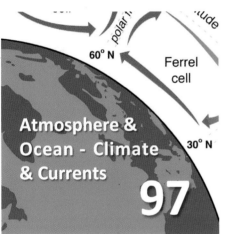
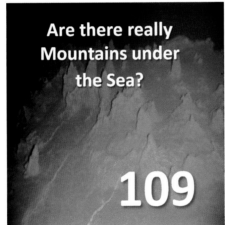

Foreword

"Making wildlife films takes me to some strange and interesting places, but when I found myself standing on a small scaffolding platform a metre above the surface of the Pacific Ocean I did wonder how much more interesting I wanted it to become, the more so when a Tiger Shark more than twice as long as me swam past an arm's length away.

These sharks gather once a year at *French Frigate Shoals*, part of the Hawaiian chain of islands, for the exact three-week period it takes for black-footed albatross chicks to leave the atoll where they've grown up. Some of the chicks leave before they can fly strongly, and they land on the lagoon where the sharks are waiting for them. Scientists had attached audio tracking tags to a few of the sharks, so we knew that one had travelled at least 600 miles to be there, possibly much further. Much about their lives is still unknown but their ability to navigate so far and to arrive every year on the first day the young albatrosses start flying suggest that the sharks have adaptations to their marine world which we can only guess at.

At a time when the human population has topped seven billion and the demands for food are at an all-time high, understanding life in the ocean has never been more important. Much of what happens at sea is scandalous and goes unreported.

Anyone who regularly goes diving or visits the ocean for other reasons can make a difference by joining organisations such as the Marine Conservation Society which campaigns for marine protection, and by taking care to discover that the fish they buy have come from sustainable sources.

In this book, Gloria Barnett gives us facts, explanations and reasons why each of us should learn more about the oceans and the crucial part they play in our world. Marvel at the wonders on display - who would have dreamed up the newly discovered Blobfish for instance - and please do your bit to make the oceans a better place."

John Aitchison

John Aitchison is a wildlife filmmaker. He's worked on many programmes for the BBC, National Geographic and Discovery Channel including Frozen Planet, Life, Big Cat Diary, The Natural World, Springwatch and Yellowstone.

Follow John's work at www.johnaitchison.net

Introduction

If you were to walk along the coastal chalk and limestone cliffs of Yorkshire and Northumberland in the United Kingdom and look towards the cold North Sea you would see fishing boats, and leisure craft bobbing along in the wind and tides. You would observe seabirds. Gannets would be diving for fish, whilst auks, puffins and guillemots would be on the cliffs below you, resting before they fly off to feed from the temperate waters. Below the waves, however, a different world exists. There are fish shoals of cod and mackerel swimming through the water and plaice hiding on the sandy bottom. There will be invertebrate species such as edible sea urchins and octopus, together with crustaceans, more commonly known as species such as lobsters and crabs. Mammals would be passing by – species of whales such as Minke, and Sei, together with orcas, dolphins, porpoise and grey seals. In the nooks and crannies of the seabed there would be strange-looking critters, such as the wolf fish, thornback rays and eels.

Cuttlefish

The seabed and rocks are either chalk reefs or rocky reefs as the Great North East Rock Reef lies just off the coast. There are rocks containing fossils of mammoth tusks and dinosaur footprints appear in the rocky sea bed giving a clue of life in a distant age. Attached to the rocks are cup corals, hydroids, deadmen's finger sponges, light bulb sea squirts and sea anemones whilst star fish scuttle across the ocean bed.

Opposite page:
Echinoderm
'Featherstar Criniod'

The water off the coast has strong currents and the Flamborough Front, where cold water from the North meets warm water from the South, gives a source of 'nutrient rich' water for over 200 miles putting food energy into the environment.

Anemone

The tiny part of the ocean world, contained in these few miles of the North Sea, is just a small example of the wonders of life which exist in the World's Oceans. If you were to observe the sea from a tropical beach or from the deck of a cruise liner crossing the oceans, you will see nothing of this strange world or the constant competition between species and the struggle for survival. This world is unseen by most humans.

The world of water is a powerful energy force which controls our climates and our decisions as to how and where we live. Oceans are essential to life on Earth, with plankton and sea grass producing 80% of our planet's oxygen supply.

Oceanography is the scientific study of our oceans and it includes Biology, Chemistry, Physics, Geology and Climatology. By beginning to understand our oceans, you enter into a fascinating world – a world of amazing life forms and adaptations for survival. You will link ideas of Earth structure with phenomenon such as mid-ocean ridges, volcanoes and tsunamis. You will be able to understand the importance of our Sun and its connection between our oceans and our atmospheric climate.

The Earth is an incredible place and with a little understanding of the science that explains our world, it becomes even more wonderful.

Welcome to the 'The Amazing World Beneath the Waves' – enjoy your journey.

Gloria Barnett
March 2021

CHAPTER ONE

The World of Water

The Earth from Space

One of the most famous pictures of our Planet, known as "Earthrise" was taken by Bill Anders from the Apollo 8 capsule in December 1968. The three-man crew of Apollo 8, Jim Lovell, Frank Borman, and Bill Anders were the first people to orbit and fly around the far side of the moon, a flight which prepared for the manned landing on the Moon in July 1969. The moon's distance from the Earth is over two hundred and thirty-eight thousand (238,000) miles.

Earthrise - NASA

Hundreds of still images were taken of Earth by astronauts during the Apollo flights but only twenty-four human beings have ever been far enough away from the planet to see the whole of the Earth travelling in space.

There are many people recorded in history who thought that the Earth was flat because they could not see it for themselves. Although Magellan first navigated the Globe in 1519-22, and scientists, even centuries earlier, had been making measurements from the surface of our Earth,

11

it was not possible to show the real shape of our Earth until there was photographic evidence from space. It is now indisputable that our Earth is a sphere flattened at the poles with a bulge at the middle – a shape known as an ellipsoid.

The famous 'Blue Marble' photograph that gave us confirmation of the shape of the Earth, is a dramatic picture with its swirling white clouds and blue water.

This picture shows our oceans clearly as vast bodies of water covering large areas of our planet. These oceans are in constant motion, influenced by the rotation of the Earth and gravitational pull of the Sun, the Moon and the Planets in our Solar System.

The Blue Marble - NASA

The World Ocean

We have documented evidence that Christopher Columbus discovered the New World in 1492 by journeying across unknown oceans and in the mid 18th century Captain James Cook did three voyages to open up the Pacific for trade. However, questions are often asked about how far the Vikings travelled on their voyages of discovery. There seems to be evidence of Vikings visiting North Atlantic islands between the 8th and 11th centuries but did they travel further? Was it the Vikings or perhaps even earlier travellers who sailed across our oceans first?

All of our oceans are part of one really large interconnected body of water, making one giant global ocean which scientists call the World Ocean. Geographically, the world ocean is split into five major oceans the Pacific, Atlantic, Indian, Southern and Arctic Oceans.

We have land – our continents and islands – yet our oceans surround it all. There are numerous smaller bodies of water known as seas or gulfs, such as the Red Sea, the Mediterranean, the Aegean and the Caribbean Sea but there is a free-flowing interchange of water throughout all of these seas and oceans. The Caribbean Islands may be a boundary between the Caribbean Sea

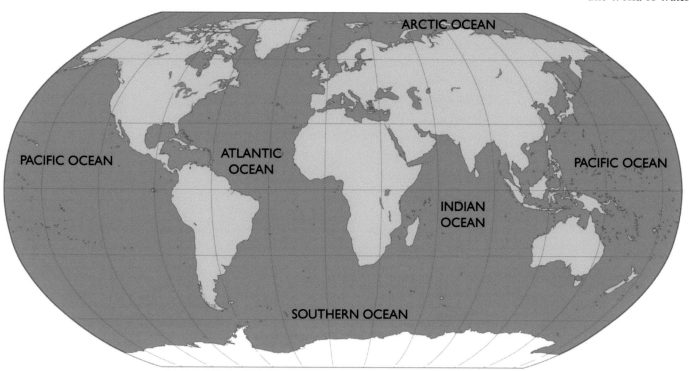

The World Ocean

and the Atlantic Ocean but the water can still flow freely around them. The Mediterranean Sea is open to the Atlantic at the Straits of Gibraltar by a mere 14 km (8.9 miles) across at its narrowest point, but this is enough for the Mediterranean to be part of the World Ocean.

Not all seas connect to the World Ocean. The Caspian Sea and Aral Sea are inland salt water seas in Asia, although the Aral Sea is presently suffering from severe drought and has very little water. Both the Caspian and Aral seas are landlocked so do not form part of our World Ocean as there is no tidal or current interchange between them and the oceans of the world.

How much water is in the Oceans?

Viewed from space the Pacific is a vast empty ocean of blue and you can hardly see land at all. The blue swathe of water covers the Earth with only a few Pacific Islands, New Zealand and Australia appearing at the bottom. The Pacific alone holds half of our World Ocean, and the Pacific, Atlantic and Indian Oceans together contain over 1300 million cubic kilometres of water.

Over 60% of the Earth is covered in water more than 100 metres deep. The deepest part of the world ocean lies at 11 kilometres below sea level, which is deeper than Mount Everest which is above sea level at a height of 8 kilometres.

Exploring the Ocean

Recreational scuba divers dive to 30 - 40 metres beneath the surface of the oceans. With more than 60% of oceans deeper than this, it means that most of our oceans are inaccessible to humans unless they use highly specialised equipment. Some recreational divers like to push themselves to the limits and train for a very specialised recreational diving certification 'Technical Diving'. The world record for a Technical Diver, diving in an immersion suit and carrying the air needed to support life, is presently just 300 metres.

This technical diver is ready to dive to a depth of 100 metres in the Red Sea.

Manned submersibles can operate at depths of 2000 metres. As complex as space shuttles, submersibles have to deal with a lack of oxygenated atmosphere, very high pressure and, of course, as they go deep, they work in complete darkness.

Only 1% of our ocean floor has been researched by man, and only one manned submersible has ever gone to the deepest part of the Ocean. A submersible took hydronauts Jacques Piccard and Don Walsh below the Pacific Ocean on January 23rd, 1960 in an area of the Pacific known as the Mariana Trench. Their ship recorded a depth of ten thousand, nine hundred and fifteen (10,915) metres. Vast research programmes are going on – but we have so much to learn. We know more about the moon and our planets than we do about our oceans. Perhaps we should consider our World Ocean to be the final frontier for scientific discovery on Earth.

The Magic of Water

The age of the Earth has been dated back to about 4.6 billion years, and geological evidence shows water has been present on the Earth's surface for more than 3.8 billion years. There is now strong agreement amongst scientists as to how water first formed on Earth, as space scientists believe that water was 'delivered' by impacts from asteroids, comets and meteorites. Ice has been proved to exist in recent meteorites which have fallen to the earth. The imported ice would have evaporated on impact and gradually formed an atmosphere of water vapour around the Earth. The Earth's atmosphere then cooled, forming clouds and rain which created the oceans.

Water is formed from two gases – hydrogen and oxygen, with the chemical formulae of H_2O. This indicates two particles of hydrogen are present for every one particle of oxygen. Once bonded together as a water molecule, these two gases then become a magical material which is the only substance on Earth which can naturally form all three 'states of matter' – a gas (steam), a liquid (water), and a solid (ice).

Although oxygen existed early in the Earth's history, it was originally only bonded with hydrogen to form water. It was some time before free-flowing oxygen gas appeared on our Earth.

Life in the Ocean

The origins of life are a complex and hotly disputed area of discussion, with scientists still making important discoveries, but there is enough evidence now to firmly understand that life began in our oceans, where one-celled (unicellular) organisms were formed.

In the history of life – more time on Earth has been recorded with just single cell organisms being present in the ocean than with the development of the rest of life on Earth. Single celled organisms were the only life on Earth for over 3 billion years out of the 4.6 billion years that Earth has existed, and these cells are the ancestors of all life forms that we know today. (One billion = 1,000,000,000). The unicellular organisms developed firstly into cells which undertook photosynthetic processes and released free oxygen on Earth, and then further development in multi-cellular organisms took place which was the beginning of the diversity of life on Earth we know now.

Life on land has been very successful, with land animals, from insects to elephants, representing 80% of all animal life, 15% of all species of animals live in the oceans, and 5% in freshwater. It is estimated that insects alone account for 80% of all species on the planet. Biodiversity is important to life on Earth, and care must be taken to protect all species whether they live on land or in water.

Environments Within the Oceans

The oceans on Earth are vast and yet there are different environments within them. There is the Big Blue, Ice World, Coral Reefs and the continental shelves around our land masses. All these areas encompass different conditions and consequently have very different life forms.

The Big Blue

The Big Blue seems to be an endless empty stretch of water, but it actually contains the largest biological environment on Earth – *'the Pelagic Realm'* – a phrase which describes the water column from the surface down to the sea bed.

The pelagic realm is divided into different zones depending on the depth.

The **Epipelagic Zone** describes the initial 200 metres below the surface. It is illuminated by sunlight which allows photosynthetic organisms to survive and algae, seagrass (the only marine plant) and most marine animals are concentrated in this zone.

The deep ocean contains vast stores of nutrients brought to the surface by a vertical movement called 'upwelling', so the upper water can also be turbid and sometimes lacks visibility due to an excess of particles in the water. This restricts the light in the zone, and only 1% of the available surface light reaches down as far as 200 metres.

The **Mesopelagic Zone** describes the area from 200 metres to 1000 metres below the surface – and is often called the Twilight Zone. Here some light penetrates but it is insufficient for photosynthesis. There is a temperature range between 0°C and 6°C and many animals have developed fluorescent adaptations to help them hunt for food. Common organisms are squid, cuttlefish and swordfish.

The **Bathypelagic Zone** lies between 1000 and 3000 metres and by this depth there is no light at all. Sperm Whales dive deep to feed on Giant Squid and there are bacteria which feed on the decomposing leftovers from dead organisms which sink down to the depths. The levels of oxygen are low due to the lack of photosynthesis in this dark and creepy zone.

The Abyssopelagic Zone is the area from 3000-4000m down to the ocean floor. It is totally dark with poor oxygen levels and most creatures are blind and colourless.

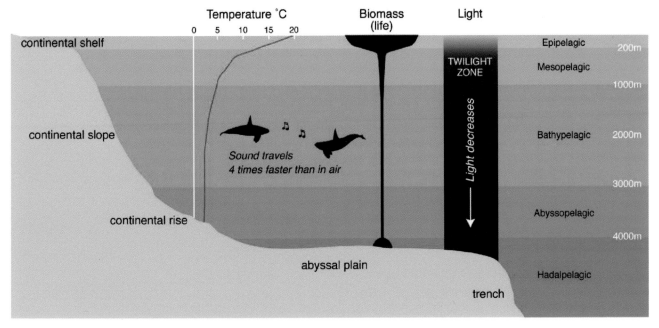

The pelagic realm

The **Hadopelagic Zone** describes the deep water in ocean trenches. This zone is mostly unknown and very few species are thought to live there, however, there have been recent discoveries of new life forms at ocean ridges and around hydrothermal vents, such as bacteria which use chemosynthesis instead of photosynthesis (the use of chemicals rather than sunlight to make food energy). The deepest part of the ocean is in the Pacific - the Mariana Trench goes to a depth of 11km but few visits by submersibles have been made to this area. The first recorded trip was in 1960, with the second trip - fifty years later. For a long time, there were more trips recorded to the Moon than manned expeditions to the deep ocean. No human has walked on the seabed at this depth at the time of writing this book.

The Ice World

A world of ice exists at both the North and South Poles, in the Arctic Ocean and the Southern Ocean, where the ice gives majestic and spectacular scenery above the seas and a strange yet beautiful silent water world beneath the ice.

Arctic Ocean Ice at Svalbard, Norway

17

Blue ice glacier at Ny Alesund, Svalbard

Glaciers & Ice Caps

Snow falling in low temperatures on land does not melt but compresses into thick ice to form glaciers. Over 10% of the land on Earth is covered by glaciation, mostly in Greenland and the Antarctic, although glaciers can be found on every continent, except Australia. Glaciers store about 70% of the world's fresh water supplies and are responsible for forming the landscape of the Earth as they grind their way overland. Glaciers in both Greenland and the Antarctic are so heavy that the land beneath them has been compressed and is now below sea level. The crystal structure of ice changes under the pressure of overlying snow and as the crystals grow, the density of the ice increases.

The downward pressure, increased density and the force of gravity make the glaciers act like rivers of ice which flow down to the sea. The blue colour which can be observed in glacial ice shows that the ice is very dense, as the ice is absorbing all other colours in the spectrum but is reflecting blue. If the ice is still white, then it is less dense and there are small air bubbles trapped in the ice and all colours are absorbed.

Glaciers can also be called ice caps. The largest ice cap is in the Antarctic, whilst the second largest covers about 80% of Greenland. The Greenland ice cap extends 2,500 km by 1,000 km and is over 1,500 m thick. Some ice at the bottom of ice caps has been estimated to be over one hundred thousand (100,000) years old.

Sea Ice

Ice is a crystalline state of water which forms on land when temperatures cool below 0°C but in seawater, due to the salt content, ice crystals only start to form at -1.8°C. Ice is initially formed on water as a film of crystals and builds up due to snowflakes falling onto the film. Ice is 10% less dense than liquid water, so when ice is formed on the water it floats rather than sinks. Sea ice gradually loses the salt from its crystalline structure and it becomes drinkable fresh water. Sea ice becomes pack ice when it loses touch with land, becomes mobile, and drifts across the surface of the ocean.

Icebergs

Icebergs are large masses of ice that calve from glaciers or ice shelves. They have been formed from snow, so they contain fresh water. The biggest, B-15, measured 11,000 square kilometres when it broke from Antarctica's Ross ice shelf in March 2000. In July 2017 an iceberg broke away from Antarctica's Larsen C ice shelf. Named A68a, this enormous iceberg followed the current around Antarctica known as "iceberg alley" and in December 2020, it was heading for the Island of South Georgia. Many scientists were worrying about the effect on the island's natural wildlife, such as penguin populations.

The most dangerous thing about icebergs is the fact that you only see 10 – 15% of the ice above water. There is nearly 90% of dangerous ice lurking beneath the surface. Some small icebergs are called growlers – this refers to icebergs which are so small they are close to the surface of the water and hard to see.

Diving in the Ice

Ice diving is described as magical due to the silence, the incredible visibility, and dramatic lighting effect however the management of the diving has to be well organised. There are dangers such as cutting the ice, and ensuring the blocks are properly lifted, or pushed away under the ice. All the normal rules such as buddy diving (never diving alone) have to be followed strenuously, and of course it is essential to have lines attached to enable the diver to find the hole again when exiting. The lines are usually kept taut so messages can be passed by pulling on the line. The divers certainly have to trust the surface support team. When you have finished your dive, wind chill can be dangerous in such low temperatures, especially when in a wet diving suit.

Ice diving to do important scientific studies is one thing – but ice diving just for recreation is another. Proper training must be organised and you must trust the dive school that is organising the trip. Ice diving is for responsible divers only, but the rewards are high with divers describing the activity as exhilarating.

CHAPTER TWO
Where Life Began

Life Begins

Most scientists have classified life today into three main groups: Archaean life; bacterial life; and everything else (animals, plants and other "eukaryotes" or things made with nucleated cells).

Archaeans (Greek for "ancient ones"), exist in regions of extreme heat and complete darkness and are known as "extremophiles".

A recent discovery of a primitive archaean microbe, deep in the Pacific Ocean at the site of a hydrothermal vent, has added further support to the idea that life on Earth began with the archaean microbes in the sea. The iron sulphide theory states that archaean bacteria originated in iron sulphide rocks around 3.5 billion years ago.

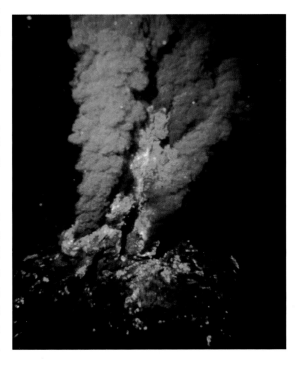

Hydrothermal Vent NOAA

Scientists had been looking for evidence of an early life form which could use the nitrogen that existed in the atmosphere or in the deep dark depths of the ocean on early Earth.

Nitrogen is an element which is an essential component of DNA, proteins and all living tissue. However, nitrogen gas, although it makes up 79% of our atmosphere, is a very unreactive, odourless and colourless gas that most forms of life cannot absorb from the atmosphere.

Scientists had long since discovered land-based nitrogen-fixing bacteria which make nitrogen usable to all other life forms when they convert the nitrogen gas into compounds such as ammonia and nitrate – but the new discovery of a single-celled organism from the depths of the ocean - the type of proto -bacteria known as "archae - indicates that nitrogen-fixing started

Opposite page: Hot springs exploding in Iceland - it is believed that life began on Earth 3.8 billion years ago in similar conditions.

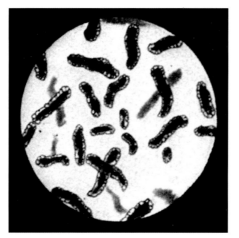

Bacteria

3.5 billion years ago - long before the three main groups diverged from one another.

This new archaean microbe is believed to have been the first form of life on the planet. Another form of bacteria, eubacteria, originated shortly after the archaean bacteria and the theory is that these two bacteria joined together to form the first eukaryotes which are the type of cells that make up all other life on Earth, including plants and animals.

Evolution of life in the oceans

Our latest discoveries tell us that one–celled organisms, found deep in the oceans, were most likely the first life on Earth 3500 million years ago (mya), and over millions of years, life existed just as these simple cells. By 3000 million years ago, however, one-celled organisms had discovered how to photosynthesise and started to release oxygen into the atmosphere, but it wasn't until 1000 million years ago that simple multicellular organisms evolved.

It is from these early, simple, multi-celled creatures that all life on earth developed. Starting with more and more complex multi-celled creatures, fish and reptiles eventually evolved between 440 – 305 mya – with today's crocodiles being very similar to early reptiles. Some fish developed legs and ventured onto land where insects, birds, dinosaurs, and mammals evolved. Some animals returned to the sea. There is even fossil evidence to show that an early species of hippopotamus returned to the sea – and evolved into the whales we have today.

Some creatures such as cnidaria (jellyfishes, hydras, sea anemones, and corals) have been on Earth for 580 million years and have been evolving ever since with over 11,000 described cnidarian species now on Earth.

Some of the organisms in the oceans have remained the same for millions of years. Sharks for example, have been on Earth for over 400 million years, long before the dinosaurs. They have not needed to evolve too much as they are a successful top predator. All of the creatures beneath them in the food webs, however, have all had to adapt and evolve to survive in their own particular niche.

Purple Anemone Coral
(Cnidaria)

The fossil record has shown how evolution has created the life we now know on Earth, both on land and in the ocean. It shows human evolution with modern humans (homo sapiens sapiens) arriving only 195 thousand years ago.

Adaptation for Survival

All marine habitats contain different species of life which have found themselves a niche in which to exist. These organisms have adapted to their own specific environment by firstly protecting themselves from predators, and secondly, ensuring that they have an accessible food supply. Adaptation can be both physical and behavioural and all adaptation processes are related to survival. It is this development of adaptations which is known as evolution.

Charles Darwin was famous for writing his Theory of Natural Selection published in 1859 that explained evolution in simple terms. Darwin's Theory created a storm when it was first published in the Victorian era as it was the first to explain that the creatures of the world had not all been created at the same time, when the world began. Up until that time, most people believed in divine intervention. Darwin however, argued that there was a natural explanation. Firstly, Darwin noticed that not all individuals in a species were identical, but some had different characteristics.

He had studied the animals on the Galapagos Islands and seen that the finches that lived on different islands had different types of beaks.

This variation in the species intrigued him. Darwin also noticed that the food supplies for the finches were different on each island and he concluded that each species of finch had adapted its beak to enable it to eat its available food. Darwin also noticed that most creatures produced more young than survived to become adults. He realised that these animals must have a struggle for existence and the animal best adapted to its environment would survive. Darwin called this idea 'survival of the fittest' and he went on to state that advantageous variations were passed on to offspring. He believed that this change occurred gradually and that over time physical adaptations could occur and new species develop.

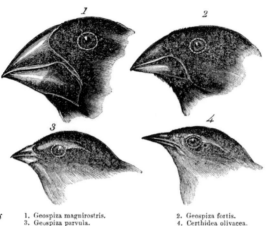

Adaptation of beaks in finches on the Galapagos Islands

1. Geospiza magnirostris.
3. Geospiza parvula.
2. Geospiza fortis.
4. Certhidea olivacea.

Darwin's Theory has since been proved to be correct by scientific understanding, especially the knowledge we have gained from the amazing discoveries in the world of genetics, which has completely endorsed all of Darwin's ideas. We have also increased our knowledge of creatures that have lived in the past and can show how animals have evolved over generations by our study of fossil records. Fossil discoveries are still being made every year as more areas of exposed rock are being studied. Recent discoveries in China have now shown the details of the evolution of birds. Birds were always thought to have evolved from dinosaurs, and now this has been proved, we are correct in our explanation of birds as the world's only living dinosaurs. Work with fossil discoveries continues daily, and evolution of most species is now proven by the fossil record.

Amazingly Darwin was working on his ideas for Natural Selection at the same time as an Austrian monk, Gregor Mendel, was working on a theory to explain the different characteristics in the pea plants which he grew in his monastery garden. Mendel is now known as the 'Father of Genetics'. Had Darwin and Mendel met, then Darwin might have been able to link his ideas with Mendel's early ideas on genetics, which could have supported his ideas on evolution.

Adaptation in Marine Life

When you study all the different types of fish in the ocean – you can see many different types of body shape. Not only do we now understand physical adaptation, but we have many different scientific studies on behavioural adaptation. The ability of fish to shoal is just one example of organisms evolving their behaviour for survival. Shoaling fish have adapted to swimming together – they do this for protection against predators. However, they have also had to adapt to sharing the available food amongst the shoal.

Goatfish, for example, will travel in a shoal – where they constantly change position with some fish on the outside to protect those fish on the inside of the shoal. Whilst on the inside some of the goatfish are filtering the sand for small edible particles using their long whiskers. The fish constantly change position. So, the shoaling is a behavioural adaptation, whilst the whiskers are a physical adaptation and both aid survival.

Goatfish shoal

Food Supplies in the Marine Environment

Almost all of life on Earth, both terrestrial and marine, use a reaction in cells called respiration to produce energy. Respiration can be explained in terms of the equation:

$$Glucose + Oxygen = Energy (ATP) + Carbon Dioxide$$

We eat food to provide the glucose and breathe in oxygen to form ATP, a chemical molecule which carries energy, and carbon dioxide, a waste product of the reaction which we eventually breathe out. A common understanding of the word respiration is just 'breathing in and out', but to biologists, respiration is the reaction which produces energy in living cells.

This means that for life on earth, breathing in oxygen, and gaining glucose from food are essential to life. The energy produced in cellular respiration is used for all activities, movement, growth, sensitivity, reproduction, feeding, excretion, and in respiration itself. Luckily respiration creates more energy in the form of ATP (adenosine triphosphate) molecules, than it uses in the process.

A few bacteria on earth use sulphur, and the archaean microbes can fix nitrogen, to produce energy instead of glucose, but these are creatures that live in extreme conditions where oxygen cannot exist.

Survival in the hostile marine environment means that food is highly important. Food supplies the glucose which runs the energy levels in organisms. All species of marine life have adapted to a life where acquisition of food is number one on their list of things to do. They spend their days or nights hiding from predators or eating. All marine life has evolved to provide different adaptations for eating a particular food source to avoid competition.

Producers and Food Chains

All food, of course, comes initially from the energy from the Sun. Photosynthesis changes light energy from the Sun into chemical energy for food. Plants photosynthesise and start off a food chain.

On land this process starts with a plant, such as grass, absorbing the light energy from the sun and using chlorophyll, carbon dioxide and water to convert light energy into oxygen and the chemical food energy of glucose. In a food chain it is the energy in the chemical glucose that is being transferred.

Food chain on land

a) Grass   b) Cow   c) Human

The arrows show the movement of the energy through the food chain.

In the sea the phytoplankton takes care of the photosynthesis and passes the food energy up the food chain to larger creatures. Plankton uses light energy to produce glucose, zooplankton eat the glucose in phytoplankton, small fish eat the glucose in zooplankton and bigger and bigger fish eat the smaller ones until you get to the top predators such as sharks.

Marine Food Chain

a) Phytoplankton   b) Zooplankton   c) Fish   d) Shark

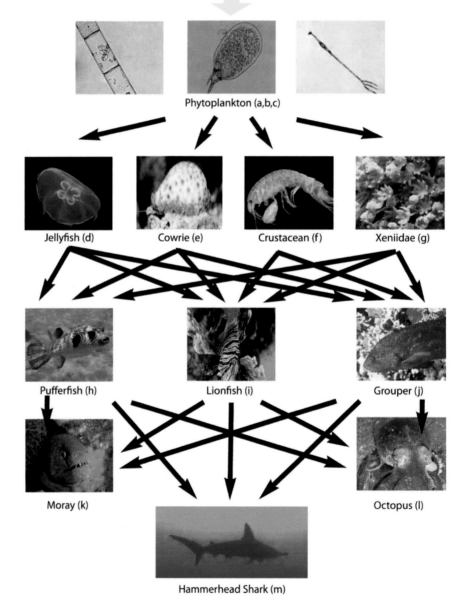

SUNLIGHT

Phytoplankton (a,b,c)

Marine Food Web

Jellyfish (d) Cowrie (e) Crustacean (f) Xeniidae (g)

Pufferfish (h) Lionfish (i) Grouper (j)

Moray (k) Octopus (l)

Hammerhead Shark (m)

Of course – life is not as simple as this, as some creatures are omnivores who eat both plant and lots of other marine organisms, and more than one species relies on a similar food source. So – food chains become food webs which describe the interrelationships between species.

Food webs are made up of interlinked food chains and can be very complex. Different organisms also use different methods of feeding. Plankton, for instance, can be scooped up using modified hairy legs, filters and baleen plates. There are filter feeders, tentacle feeders, detritus feeders, grazers and predators. All have their place in the food webs of the ocean.

Oxygen in the Oceans

Most life in the marine environment relies on oxygen and glucose to fuel their energy supply. The glucose is readily available in the form of the food chains, but oxygen levels in the ocean are low. Sea water contains only 1% dissolved oxygen (5 parts per million), compared to 20% oxygen in the atmosphere (210,000 ppm). Sea life has therefore had to adapt special body parts to deal with the low oxygen levels. Fish have developed gills. Fish don't breathe in and out but have a constant flow of water over the gills, which have a large surface area to absorb oxygen into the blood. If humans were to 'breathe' water, we would need 450 breaths per minute to get an equivalent amount of oxygen into our bodies. Sharks have 5 gills on each side of their body and they mainly force water over their gills by swimming. There is, however, one shark - the six gilled shark - which lives deep in the ocean and has developed an extra gill filament on each side of its body. The extra gill increases the surface area for water to pass over and enables the shark to absorb more oxygen from water than it would if it only had 5 gills. As oxygen content in sea water decreases with depth this extra gill is a very good adaptation for survival.

Some creatures have not developed specialised organs for extracting oxygen from water, and they surface to breathe oxygen from the atmosphere. Whales, dolphins, and turtles are amongst these creatures. Some whales can remain below water for two hours when hunting, whilst a Blue Whale is thought to surface every 30-40 minutes. Turtles can remain below water for up to six hours.

CHAPTER THREE

Life in the Oceans

The oceans of the world are home to representatives of most groups of animal in the classification system of life on earth from the Blue Whale - the largest creature on Earth to diatoms which are microscopic one-celled life forms. There is a Census of Marine Life being conducted around the world which has recorded over 15,000 species of fish and over 200,000 other marine species. Estimates are that the total number could be up to 2 million species of life living in the ocean environment.

As you will see from the table below – only insects and amphibians are missing from the Ocean ecosystem.

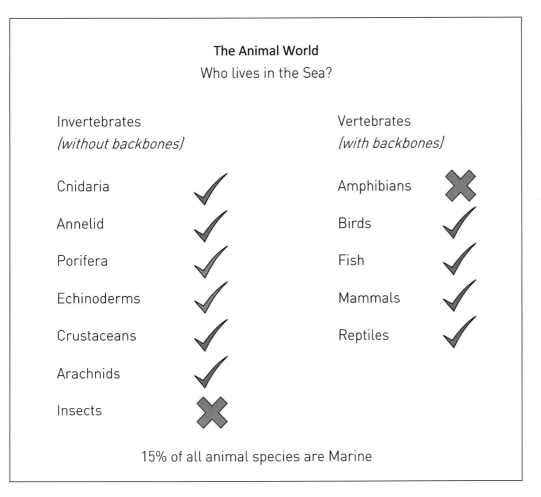

The Animal World

Who lives in the Sea?

Invertebrates (without backbones)		Vertebrates (with backbones)	
Cnidaria	✓	Amphibians	✗
Annelid	✓	Birds	✓
Porifera	✓	Fish	✓
Echinoderms	✓	Mammals	✓
Crustaceans	✓	Reptiles	✓
Arachnids	✓		
Insects	✗		

15% of all animal species are Marine

Opposite page: Sponges are invertebrate animals which have been in the oceans for over 150 million years. (Phylum: Porifera)

31

The Five Kingdoms

Scientists like to classify life – they put creatures into different 'boxes' depending on their cell and body structure. We call the first level of classification 'Kingdoms'. There is a Kingdom for Bacteria, Fungi, Protoctista, Plants and Animals and all five of these groups are represented in the marine environment.

- Bacteria which use chemicals, such as hydrogen sulphide, live deep in the ocean and have been found at high temperatures near hydrothermal vents.

- Fungi have been found in deep sea sediments in the Indian Ocean. Fungi is often found growing on sponges.

- Protoctista – are probably the most important kingdom in the oceans as they photosynthesise. They can be free floating phytoplankton, multicelled algae such as seaweed and kelp, or algae which live within coral and fish

- Plants exist mainly on land, and the only true plant in the sea is seagrass which lives in the shallow waters of continental shelves.

- The Animal Kingdom. Although it is easy to get mixed up between animals and mammals, the Animal Kingdom is made up of groups such as Reptiles, Mammals, Fish, Birds, Frogs, Spiders, and Insects. All the animals without backbones such as lobsters, starfish and worms are invertebrates, whilst other animals which have a backbone are called vertebrates. Mammals are vertebrates and even though they exist in different forms such as humans and whales, they are just one class of animal within the Animal Kingdom.

The Bacteria Kingdom

Bacteria can be found throughout the marine world. They are useful to their environment as they are mostly decomposers which breakdown organic matter. The ocean floor provides a good source of organic matter for them to feed on. There are also specialised bacteria which harness the nitrogen which is present in the oceans. These bacteria use nitrogen fixing reactions to absorb ammonia produced as a waste product of other marine species of life.

One group of microorganisms are the Archaea which were first accepted into scientific classification in the 1980s. These organisms live in extreme conditions and they obtain their energy by reacting with methane and sulphide compounds rather than with oxygen. Archaea can survive in extremes such as the high salinity of the Dead Sea, or the high temperature areas of deep-sea vents.

Bioluminescence is the biochemical emission of light. A green light is often seen when disturbing the surface water at night and this is caused by the bacteria *Vibrio fischeri* which is floating through the water feeding on dead organic matter. Luminescent bacteria also live within the bodies of deep-sea creatures. The bacteria gains protection whilst the deep-sea organisms can use bioluminescent lures to attract their prey. This type of relationship is known as a symbiotic relationship, where two organisms live closely together and help each other to survive.

The Fungi Kingdom

It has been estimated that there are over 1500 species of marine fungi. They often act as decomposers, breaking down dead organic matter, and are found in symbiotic relationships. Very little is known about the diversity of marine fungi and there is a need to study more areas of the marine environment to establish further understanding of their importance.

Some isolated studies have been conducted, and one study found 681 different fungal strains could be isolated from just 16 sponge species. Sponges only exist in the marine environment and harvesting useful strains of fungi from sponges could be a scientific endeavour for the future.

The Protoctista Kingdom

Protoctista are tiny, microscopic organisms which are essential to life on Earth.

Diatoms in Antarctica

One litre of sea water can contain 15,000 of these small organisms - known as diatoms . They are about 2 microns thick – which is about a hair's width and they float in the currents in the upper 10 - 15 metres of the oceans. Diatoms can be found in cold water whilst their close relatives, the dinoflagellates, live in warm water. There are many species of these organisms and they are known collectively as phytoplankton.

Phytoplankton are delicate unicellular algae that contain a small yellow brown or green chloroplast structure that contains the important chemical 'chlorophyll'. It is chlorophyll which is responsible for probably the most important chemical reaction for life on Earth – photosynthesis.

Photosynthesis converts light energy to chemical energy by using chlorophyll and light energy from the Sun. Inorganic molecules such as carbon dioxide gas, and liquid water are converted into the life-giving chemical glucose in an amazing chemical reaction which gives off oxygen gas as the waste product.

Carbon Dioxide + Water (using chlorophyll and light) turns into Glucose + Oxygen

What happens to the glucose and oxygen?

The glucose forms oil droplets which are rich in energy and this chemical energy enters the food chain. The production of oxygen in photosynthesis produces free oxygen gas. All living creatures use oxygen to burn the glucose in 'respiration' which occurs in every living cell, and this reaction makes the energy molecules needed for life on Earth to exist.

Land plants have long been called the lungs of the world due to their photosynthetic abilities to convert carbon dioxide to oxygen, yet plants only make about 20% of the oxygen present in the atmosphere. It is estimated that 10% of oxygen is produced by sea-grass living in the oceans, and over 70% of the world's supply of oxygen comes from the ocean's phytoplankton.

Algae

Algae is also a member of the Protoctista Kingdom. It occurs in two main forms in the marine environment - multicelled algae (lots of cells) or unicellular algae (one cell). Blue-green unicellular algae (commonly known as cyanobacteria) are traditionally the oldest and simplest of the algae. However, some scientists prefer to exclude cyanobacteria from Algae classification due to differences in their structure, especially the lack of a chloroplast, which is where photosynthesis takes place in multicelled algae and plants. Whether they are classified as bacteria or algae, the importance of cyanobacteria is immense, as is shown in the fossil record.

Our earliest fossils contain colonies of cyanobacteria (also known as blue-green algae) and they are thought to have formed stromatolites over 2.8 billion years ago. The blue-green algae were able to photosynthesise without a chloroplast, and used just a thin membrane, a thylakoid membrane, to create the glucose and oxygen. It was these blue-green algae which were responsible for the oxygenation of the atmosphere. This oxygenation of the earth allowed evolution to begin so we can all trace our ancestors back to the blue-green algae that existed so long ago. The importance to life on earth of the early algae cannot be over-emphasised, and we can still see their ancestors now, as the marine environment is full of microscopic algae which still have an important job to do today.

Coccolithophores, for instance, are microscopic algae that build an outside skeleton of calcium carbonate. They float in the surface of the oceans and capture carbon dioxide from the atmosphere which is stored in their skeleton. When they die, they sink – and trap the carbon in the ocean. The activity of these small algae plays a large part in preventing the Greenhouse Effect, where carbon dioxide gas is increasing in the Earth's atmosphere. Recent research has found that the coccolithophores are getting bigger, and thus trapping more CO_2 from the atmosphere every year.

Red Sea coral containing zooxanthellae

So nearly three billion years ago cyanobacteria created the gas oxygen in our atmosphere which helped to create life, whilst today, coccolithophores are removing an excess gas which is threatening life on earth. Clever little things – unicellular algae!

The most studied case of an algae living in a symbiotic relationship in the marine environment is the unicellular zooxanthellae. These algae live within the coral providing the oxygen and absorbing waste from the coral. It helps the coral to build its calcareous skeleton.

The coral supplies the zooxanthellae with nutrients and protects it from the harsh environment. The added benefit to all organisms sharing space with bacteria is the added colour which the bacteria imparts. The beautiful colour of corals is due to the relationship between the coral and microscopic zooxanthellae.

The Sailor's eyeball algae. This is a one celled organism.

There is also one unicellular algae which is quite spectacular the wonderful and imaginatively named Sailor's Eyeball (*Ventricaria ventricosa*) which is one of the largest single-celled organisms on Earth. It grows into a ball shape up to 6cm across. It is a single huge cell with a dark green liquid filled centre. Who could believe that algae could be so beautiful?

35

The multicellular algae first occurred on Earth some two billion years later than unicellular algae. Multicellular algae can be found in various colours – blue, green, brown, and red. It grows as slime, in clusters, as ribbons, and on stalks. It forms large structures of seaweed and kelp. It often looks like a plant – and often gets mistakenly described as a plant, as of course, it does what a plant is famous for – it photosynthesises. Free living algae have some wonderful names, brown slime, green-glove mat, jelly tuft, sponge ball, chain and glob-weed. Giant seaweeds form structures called holdfasts which enable it to cling on to rocks and this is particularly useful in tidal situations where the seaweed needs to remain in the water to avoid desiccation, rather than being swept up onto a beach in strong tides.

The Plant Kingdom

Over 350,000 living species of plants can be found on Earth today. There are plants of all types, colours and structures from flowering plants to meat eating plants, and some plants which are parasitic (living off a host organism), but they all have one thing in common – they are all photosynthetic. They can be found everywhere on land from forests to the top of mountains – they are the producers in our food chains and support all life on earth. In the oceans, however, there is only one species of real plant to be found – Seagrass.

Seagrass Meadow in Philippines

Seagrass is a vascular plant (it contains tubes for transfer of internal liquids) and has roots and ribbon-like leaves. Some species have distinct stems whilst others have underground roots called rhizomes. Seagrass uses light in photosynthesis to produce energy and therefore is found in the shallow photic (light) zone in the top 30 metres of the sea where light is available, although there are some areas of the world where the sea is so clear they can be found up to 200m below the surface. Seagrass helps to stabilize sediments and the meadows also act as nurseries for many animal species. Seagrass traps nutrients from the water such as the phytoplankton which floats through the ocean and it is also a producer at the start of the ocean food chain. It is a major food source for herbivorous animals such as snails, sea urchins, fish, manatees, dugongs (a strange marine mammal) and turtles.

Mangroves

Mangroves contain different species of tree which live in the intertidal zone. They survive desiccation when the tide is out and flooding when the tide is in. They usually have their roots submerged in water with varying salt concentrations from brackish water, with a low salt content, to full ocean salinity of 35 grams of salty chemicals per litre. Mangrove has adapted to removing salt with specialised filtration processes in its roots and leaves and has special adaptations for obtaining oxygen and for reproduction.

Mangrove is an important marine habitat as it provides food and shelter for many species. It acts as a nursery for juvenile fish, provides nutrients from falling leaves, and stabilises sediments. Mudflats within the mangroves are habitats for crabs and mudskippers whilst the canopy of the mangrove is a habitat for nesting birds.

Mangrove in the Florida Everglades

The Animal Kingdom

Obviously, humans are animals who have not adapted to live in a marine environment. We have large air spaces in our bodies, and large lungs which do not take oxygen from water. We can swim only at restricted depths because our bodies cannot cope with the pressure of the water which increases around us the deeper we descend. There is also a real danger of death from decompression sickness if too much nitrogen builds up in the blood.

Recreational scuba divers regularly dive to 30-40 metres – but to do that they need:

- fins to give them power and speed in the water
- masks to protect their eyes
- weights to get them down
- buoyancy jackets to keep them from sinking too deep
- immersion suits to protect from the cold and
- breathing apparatus connected to a tank of air.

Human beings have not adapted to a life under the water – so divers have to take all of their survival equipment with them. Modern diving is much safer due to the increased efficiency of wetsuits and SCUBA equipment. (Scuba stands for self-contained underwater breathing apparatus).

Diver in full scuba kit in the murky waters of Scapa Flow

Marine Animals

There are two major groups of animals – invertebrates (without backbones) and vertebrates (with backbones), and species from both of these groups are found in the ocean.

Marine Invertebrates

Invertebrates are animals without backbones, and these are divided up into other biological 'boxes' such as Phylum, e.g. cnidaria, molluscs, echinoderms, sponges, worms, and arthropods. Arthropods can be further sub-divided into crustaceans, arachnids and insects. Species of all these invertebrate phylum, except insects, can be found in the oceans.

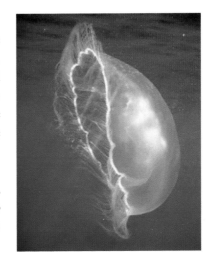

Moon Jellyfish – a Cnidarian

Cnidaria are a large and diverse group including hydroids, jellyfish, anemones and corals. Over 9,000 species have so far been identified. They are the oldest multicellular animals – with fossils first appearing 550 million years ago.

Molluscs have been around for 540 million years and are highly developed within their invertebrate structure. Molluscs have organs such as a heart, gills, intestines and stomachs as well as eyes and a nervous system. They can be divided into snails, bivalves such as clams and cephalopods (squid and octopus) and are the second largest animal phylum on Earth. Molluscs are the largest marine phylum comprising about 23% of all the named marine organisms. 5,000 species of molluscs have been identified on the Great Barrier Reef in Australia.

A Giant Clam is a mollusc

Echinoderms are exclusively marine animals. They first appeared 500 million years ago (mya) and presently there are over 6,500 species. They have a unique radially symmetrical body but lack a brain or heart. They use water pressure to power movement and despite having no backbone some species do use skeletal plates arranged

radially under their skin, often with spines for protection. Echinoderms are creatures such as crinoids, starfish and sea cucumbers.

Sponges – are simple multicellular animals and fossil sponge reefs have been found which are more than 450 million years old. Sponges are filter feeders, absorbing nutrients from the water. A beach ball sized sponge can filter up to two tonnes of water per day as it passes through tiny pores to a network of internal canals.

Worms – flatworms, annelids (round worms), nemotodes, and ribbon worms all exist in the marine environment with over 17 different phyla being known. They were the first animals to develop bilateral symmetry and are likely to be an ancestor of all higher animals. Bilateral symmetry is where a line can be drawn down the middle of the creature to create a mirror image on either side.

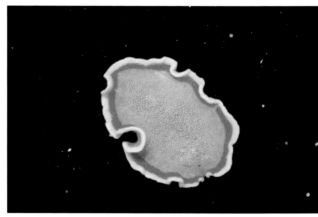

Arthropod means 'jointed legs' and includes the classes of crustaceans, arachnids (spiders), millipedes and insects. They use 'chitin' which is a skeletal type substance to form exoskeletons (outside skeletons) for protection. They evolved in marine waters 350 mya and more than 50,000 species now exist in the marine environment.

Insects evolved from an original marine species which transferred to land and there are now millions of species of insects. There are no insects which have colonised the seas, although Marine flies live on the surface and the larva of a small number of flies and beetles live beneath the surface, in rock pools.

Arthropods - tiny cleaner shrimps hide in an anemone coral

Marine Vertebrates

Vertebrates are creatures with backbones and are commonly recognised as Amphibians, Birds, Fish, Mammals and Reptiles. There are a few toads which live in brackish environments such as mangrove swamps, but there are no true sea dwelling amphibians.

Although no bird lives entirely in the marine environment, sea birds cannot exist without food from the oceans. Albatross, for example, can remain in the air from 2 to 4 years feeding from the oceans, and land only to roost. Penguins are the most physically adapted bird for a marine lifestyle being streamlined and graceful in the water, whilst they are cumbersome and comical on land.

Fish are only adapted for their watery existence, yet there are species of reptiles and mammals which have conquered both a land and a marine existence. Sea snakes are reptiles which are fully adapted for their marine life, whilst turtles and iguanas still need to use land for some parts of their lifestyles. Turtles, for instance, return to lay eggs on sandy beaches, while Marine Iguanas only enter the sea to find their food.

Mammals such as whales and dolphins, collectively known as Cetaceans, can be found only in the oceans. Whales and dolphins are air breathing creatures, so have to return to the surface regularly to breathe. They exchange carbon dioxide for the oxygen needed to make the energy they expend when travelling far and wide in the marine ecosystem. Dolphins and humans seem to share an affinity which may be based on our shared intelligence but there is more research to be conducted before we can fully understand their system of whistles and clicks and actually share communication with these fascinating creatures.

Dolphin

CHAPTER FOUR

Life at the Bottom - Life at the Top

Creatures from the Deep

These creatures have become highly adapted for their dark, high pressure and low oxygen environment. Many creatures have developed light producing organs called photophores. These use bioluminescent bacteria to produce strange lights in the dark which confuses predators or attracts food. Several deep-sea species can lower their metabolic rate so they need less oxygen to produce energy. Some creatures are just weird and wonderful.

There are countless strange deep-sea creatures in the world's oceans here are just a few of those that have been discovered so far.

Gulper Eels can be found at a depth of 1.8km and are a cross between a snake and a pelican – the jaw unhinges like a snake to swallow large prey and it has a pelican like pouch as a mouth. It can grow up to 2 metres long and its head is one quarter of its body size. Its tail is tipped with a luminous bulb shaped photophore, and it can eat fish the same size as itself.

Gulper Eel - Saccopharynx

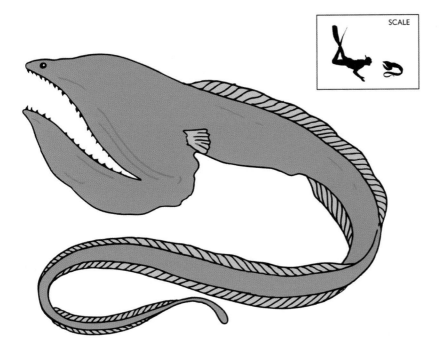

SCALE

The Anglerfish is the size of a beach ball, with terrifying teeth. When it opens its mouth, it creates a strong inward suction. It has a photophore lure on the top of its head and an expanding stomach to store large fish. Its skin is brown – which at depth makes it completely invisible. The male is tiny, just the size of a golf ball. It makes its home over 1km below the surface.

Far Right: Anglerfish

Vampire Squid (*vampyroteuthis infernalis* translates as 'vampire squid from hell'.) Usually found between 600 - 1,200 metres where oxygen levels are low. It feeds on small crustaceans such as prawns but although it is big enough to envelope your head it is considered to be harmless to humans. Its adaptations for the deep include a low rate of metabolism which enables it to survive in the low oxygen conditions, and photophores on its body to attract food.

Right: Vampire Squid

The Oarfish may be responsible for the serpent tales in maritime folklore as they linger at the surface when sick or dying. Their highly compressed, elongated bodies are the longest of the bony fish in our oceans with some specimens being recorded at over 15 metres. To give you some idea of what that length means to a diver – just take a look at the size of the fish and diver on the scale at the top of the oarfish diagram.

Far Right: Oarfish

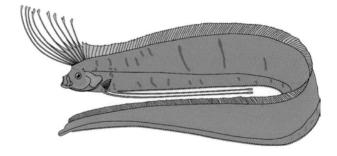

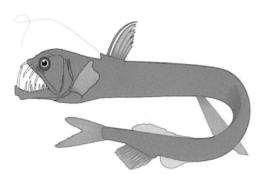

The Viper Fish is a nasty fish considering it is so small (30 cm long). Its teeth are so large they extrude from its mouth. It flashes its photophore to attract prey and has a shock absorber in its neck to protect it as it attacks its prey at speed. It has a low metabolic rate to deal with the lack of oxygen at 1.5km below the surface. Some species are thought to be able to swim at an incredible two body lengths per second.

Far left: Viper Fish

Fangtooth holds the record for the largest teeth in proportion to its body size. It has two enormous fangs in the lower jaw which slide into pockets in the roof of its mouth. However, at a mere 16cm it should not be feared by humans too much.

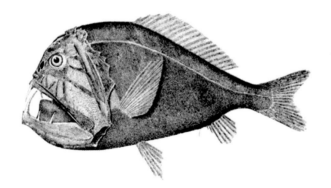

Left: Fangtooth

The Hagfish is not a true fish as it has no backbone but it is a member of the Animal Kingdom. This little monster is found at over 1.2 km down and has the reputation of being quite disgusting. It can produce a fibre-filled slime to cover its body for protection whilst it feeds by boring into its prey and sucking out the flesh. They live on the deep-sea bottom, and often hide in the sand.

Far Left: Atlantic Hagfish

45

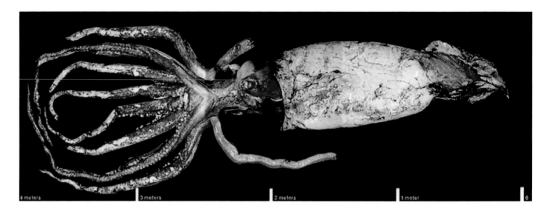

This Giant Squid measures over 4 metres (13 ft)

The Giant Squid is a deep-sea cephalopod, a member of the Mollusc phylum. The first photograph of a live Giant Squid in the ocean was only taken in 2006 as they were so hard to find, due to the depths in which they live. They are known as voracious solitary hunters with a powerful beak and they have strong tentacles to catch their prey. It is thought that these squid prefer mid-latitude ocean temperatures as no specimen has yet been found at the poles. Scientists are still researching just how deep these amazing creatures will travel and there is evidence of them in the water column between 300m and 1 km beneath the waves. Giant Squid are the regular food choice of Sperm Whales.

Far Right: Giant Isopod

The Giant Isopod is related to a woodlouse. The largest yet found weighed 1.7 kg, and measured 30 cm. It can be found at depths of 2 km from the surface. It is believed to have developed 'deep sea gigantism' which is thought to help the creature deal with the intense pressures whilst living at depths. This isopod is a carnivore and will eat anything – including the carcasses from dead whales.

Right: Blobfish

Recently discovered in Australia, the Blobfish has been found at depths of over 800m. The adaptations of this creature are quite amazing – instead of a gas filled buoyancy bladder like most fish, the Blobfish is a mass of 'jelly' with a density slightly less than that of water – so it can float over the sea floor. About 30 cm in length, the blob fish is in danger of extinction due to deep sea fishing methods.

Adaptation at the top of the ocean

Let's move away from the depths of the ocean and have a closer look at the creatures which inhabit the waters nearer the surface.

Plankton are organisms whose movements in the ocean are determined by ocean currents. There are two main types: phytoplankton and zooplankton.

Bacteria are the most abundant of species in the world, but coming a close second are the planktonic species. Some estimates of the total amount of biomass created by plankton are larger than the total biomass of all fish, sharks and whales. Not a bad statistic for such tiny creatures.

Phytoplankton

In the ocean, the organisms which photosynthesise, are phytoplankton. Their name comes from 'phyto', the Greek word for 'plant', and 'planktos' which means 'drifter' or 'wanderer' and their importance lies in the fact that these simple one-celled organisms can float near the surface in order to obtain the light needed for photosynthesis. These creatures are the primary producers in the oceanic food chain. There are thousands of different species of phytoplankton and they can be very different in appearance. Phytoplankton can come in many different shapes and sizes

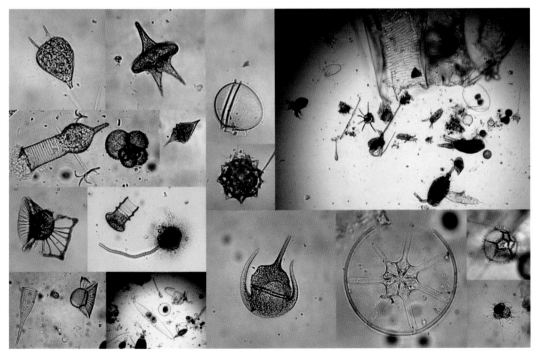

A variety of phytoplankton

47

they can be needle shaped, star shaped, have spiralling cells or form chains using claspers and congregate into colonies. Some have spiny projections which help them to float and avoid sinking away from the light. This collage of microscope photographs was prepared by an Oceanographic research scientist.

You will need a microscope to see the individual phytoplankton cells, but when grouped together they may appear to discolour the water. When phytoplankton 'blooms' are green this is to the presence of a photosynthetic pigment called chlorophyll, whilst brown or red blooms show the presence of 'accessory' pigments. Some blooms of plankton are so large they can be seen from space.

Red plankton blooms can sometimes cause health risks to marine organisms. Fish feeding from a bloom which contains a toxic red plankton will eat the poisonous plankton, and pass the toxin into the food chain, on to larger marine life and possibly even to humans. It is believed that toxic plankton was the cause of death of 14 humpback whales in Cape Cod Bay in 1987, and a red plankton caused coral mortality in the Persian Gulf in 2010. Only a handful, out of the thousands of different species of phytoplankton, are known to be toxic.

Zooplankton

As well as phytoplankton floating at the surface of the oceans, there are also tiny animals, the zooplankton. These creatures eat phytoplankton, material from dead organisms or anything edible which is floating around in the water that is small enough to digest. Zooplankton rely on the ocean currents and tides to be transported to areas where nutrients are available. Zooplankton refers to a broad category of creatures which can vary in size from microscopic single-celled organisms to larger multi-celled creatures. Scientists know very little about the one-celled radiolarians, but agree that the important phylums of cnidarians, jellyfish, copepods and krill can be included as planktonic organisms, and they are a vital part of the food chain. Zooplankton can also include the larvae and eggs of larger marine animals.

Copepods

One of the major providers of protein in the ocean are the zooplankton species, copepods. They are members of the phylum arthropods and are tiny crustaceans. Over 13,000 species of copepods have been described, and there are more planktonic copepods than any other species of zooplankton. They are the major food source for small fish, krill, seabirds and baleen whales.

Copepod

Copepods are amazing little creatures. Many feed near the surface at night, but return to deeper water during daylight hours to avoid predators. They are considered to be a major part of the carbon cycle as their faeces, and waste gas from respiration give out carbon dioxide and they can move carbon from the surface to the deeper sea environment.

Copepods can be 1 to 2 mm long, with an elongated oval shaped body and two pairs of large antennae. Their body is almost totally transparent. Copepods have a compound, single red eye, in the centre of the head. As they are so small, copepods have no need of any heart or circulatory system and most lack gills as they are adapted to absorbing oxygen directly into their bodies. One pair of antennae is used like oars to move the animal through the water. Some copepods can move extremely fast over a few millimetres in order to escape from predators, and if you were to compare a copepod with a cheetah in terms of size then the copepod would be extremely fast and move at the equivalent speed of over 3,000 km per hour.

Krill

Krill are small crustaceans that feed on phytoplankton and zooplankton, and then get eaten by larger creatures such as fish and squid. Krill makes up the main diet of one type of whale, and are considered a tasty titbit for seals and penguins.

CHAPTER FIVE

The Coral Reef Community

Coral Reefs are among the largest and most spectacular structures on Earth. Large reefs such as the Great Barrier Reef of Australia can even be seen from space.

The Great Barrier Reef is the largest coral reef system in the world and is made up of 2,500 different reefs around 850 islands. This coral reef has gone through a series of 'lives' with alternate periods of growth and destruction and although the reef has been known to exist for over 500,000 years, its Australia present structure is quite young at about 8,000 years old. It presently measures about two and a half thousand kilometres long, has an area totalling 350 thousand square kilometres and is approximately one fifth of all the reef structures on Earth.

The Great Barrier Reef is the largest marine park in the world and was made a World Heritage site in 1981. It has been labelled by some as one of the Seven Wonders of the Modern World.

An enormous diversity of species from unicellular algae to white tip sharks live in the coral reef environment where the reef provides an ideal habitat for marine organisms as they find food and shelter on the reef.

Left: Diversity of life in the coral reef

Importance of Coral Reefs

Although coral reefs are only 0.25% of the total marine environment in the Earth's oceans, they actually give a home to over 25% of aquatic life. Thousands of different species live together in the ocean equivalent of 'cities' and there is constant competition for space and food. Reefs are found in over 110 countries around the world, where they form islands and protect shorelines from erosion. There are three main types of reef – Atoll, Barrier and Fringing Reefs.

Far left: Typical Coral Reef

Coral Atoll

An atoll is formed near the surface of the sea, and it is separated from an island by a lagoon. The atoll extends around the lagoon in a circular structure.

Barrier Reef

Barrier reefs grow at large distances offshore, parallel to the coast, whilst a Fringing Reef borders the coast more closely, often being separated by only a narrow stretch of water.

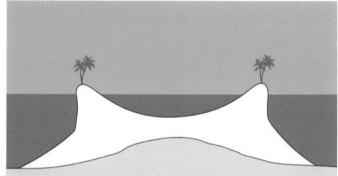

Fringing Reef

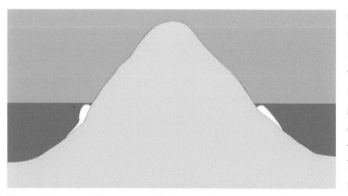

Coral reefs only exist beneath the waves, and are mainly found in shallow, clear and warm tropical marine oceans. A tropical coral reef ecosystem is an incredibly stable environment – there is reduced wave movement compared to a beach and little change in salinity. There are no tidal fluctuations and few seasonal changes in average water temperature, daylight hours and intensity of light. It is this stability which allows millions of different species of life to coexist in this most beautiful and complex ecosystem on Earth. Coral Reefs are believed to be the most biodiverse ecosystem on Earth with over 80% of all known animal phyla present within their environment.

Cnidarians

Coral is a living organism, a cnidarian, which is an invertebrate animal. Coral reefs are made of different species of cnidarians, which exist as tiny polyps of delicate cup-shaped bodies.

Cnidarians are a large and diverse group in the Animal Kingdom. They are an ancient group that first appeared on Earth over 550 million years ago and there are presently over 10,500 described species. All are aquatic and live in the marine environment.

Cnidarians include hydroids, hydrozoans, jellyfish, anemones and scleractinia – the corals. The word cnidarian comes from the Greek 'cnidos' which means stinging needle – and a common feature of all the cnidarians is the nasty sting which you can get from hydroids, anemones, jellyfish and corals. All of the reef building (hermatypic) species of coral live together and form colonies which build up the structure of the coral reef.

Types of Coral

There are two major types of coral – hard coral and soft coral. Hard coral is made up of individual cnidarian cup polyps or corallites which build calcium carbonate skeletons around themselves for protection.

Hard and Soft Coral

Soft coral usually has no cup structure but often has a hydro-skeleton of water which fills the inside of the coral and exerts water pressure from the inside, thus giving shape to the colony of coral polyps.

There are many species of cnidarian which make up both soft and hard coral – but all are filter feeders which extract nutrients such as phytoplankton which are floating past in the water.

Corals are all small sessile creatures which sit and wait for their food to come to them. There are many spectacular species of hard coral: finger corals, staghorn corals, dome, mushroom, bubble, honeycomb and brain coral. There are corallites which fuse together, and coral with laminae structures and toothed edges such as the Elephant Ear coral.

53

Soft coral is the common name for the class of animal Anthozoa – which have soft polyps such as slimy leather coral or gorgonian fans. Napththeidae have a hydro-skeleton, whilst Xeniidae have large feathery leaf-like tentacles which pulsate rhythmically about 40 times a minute to create a current to help feeding and respiration. There are giant sea fans, sea whips, sea pens, wire coral, and sea anemones which can carpet the hard coral and provide shelter for wonderfully coloured anemone fish and shrimps which are immune to their stings. Corals take a long time to grow into a reef structure, and individual corals – such as a Gorgonian Sea Fan can have up to 500 years of growth on one structure.

Right: Soft Coral Red Sea

Far Right Top: Bubble Anemone Soft coral with resident anemone fish

Far Right Bottom: Xeniidae – a coral which pulsates to filter the water for plankton

How hard coral forms a reef structure

Hard coral provides the building blocks for a coral reef and forms in three stages – firstly, the growth of individual polyps, secondly, the building of a calcium carbonate skeleton around the polyps, and then cementation between polyps creating the reef structure. The calcium carbonate in the water comes from the shells and skeletons of decomposing sea creatures and from the absorption by the sea of carbon dioxide. Calcium carbonate is also returned to the environment when a reef is damaged by wave action or bio-erosion of the reef by grazing fish. The skeletal material builds up over a long period of time and over thousands of generations of cnideria. Cementation between polyps is a continuous process both by coralline algae and other organisms with fish supplying nitrogen from the urea in their faeces. It is these nitrogenous substances which supply the 'glue' to cement the reef.

Coral polyps are invertebrates which have a cup-shaped radial symmetry with a mouth, stomach and stinging tentacles. The polyp is a hollow sac with the single opening at the top which acts as both the mouth and anus. The tentacles sway in the water, using stinging cells to help to paralyse the plankton and other nutrients. The tentacles then contract to move the food into the sac. The polyps are very simple organisms with a decentralised and very basic nervous system. They are sessile organisms, meaning they do not chase their food, but stay in one place filtering the water for food.

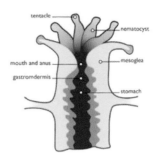

Structure of a Coral Polyp

Coral polyps work symbiotically, in a helpful relationship, with the algae zooxanthellae which live within the polyp. The photosynthetic algae provide the products of photosynthesis – the oxygen and glucose for the coral, whilst the coral provides protection and availability to light for the algae. It is the algae within the polyp which gives the corals all their different colours.

Cup Coral

Some species of coral, e.g. fire coral, produce toxins which stop them being overgrown – unfortunately they can also use this chemical warfare to give a diver a very nasty sting if they happen to brush their skin on the coral.

55

Top Left: Great Star Hard Coral

Top Centre: Brain Hard Coral

Top Right: Acropora Hard Coral

Bottom: Hard Corals in the Red Sea

Reefs under threat

Although reef structures have been in existence for over 450 million years, the original blue green algae colonies have long since been replaced by the hermatypic coral we have today, which was first formed 190 million years ago.

Coral Reefs, however, are under threat. They are in crisis and dying at an incredible speed throughout the world. An estimated quarter of all coral reefs have disappeared in the last few decades, and the reefs in South East Asia, which are the most species-rich reefs in the world, are at serious risk. A recent study of the reefs in the Florida Keys shows a decline of more than 9 out of 10 of the species previously recorded. The reason for such an appalling decline in reef health is mainly human activity. Humans have affected the reefs by pollution, overfishing, dynamite and cyanide fishing and extraction of healthy coral for the tourist trade. Coral has also been bleached due to the rise in ocean temperatures, due mainly to the increase of carbon dioxide in our atmosphere, caused by both natural and human activity.

The reef environment can be damaged when there is a change in the ecological balance of species living on the reef. Changes in the food chain create all sorts of ecological havoc. There has to be a fine balance between the numbers of predators and the creatures which they eat in order to maintain the health of the reef.

Coral is always under threat, and of the 7,500 corals species that we have discovered as once living on this Earth, over 5,000 species are now extinct. Coral has survived many mass extinctions, but the most recent problems are happening at a much faster rate, leaving little time for recovery. When reefs are threatened with disease and environmental damage it could destroy the fine ecological relationships and the reefs could be lost forever.

Diversity of Reef Life

There are hard and soft corals of all shapes and sizes, there are algae, sponges, worms, crustaceans, and snails. There are fish and turtles – and so many other organisms living in this vast and diverse food web. Over 25% of all marine life lives in a coral reef ecosystem. Coral reefs contain many habitats, and all creatures find their own niche within the coral environment. Life forms, from unicellular algae through consumer levels to the highest level of predator, all rely on the reef for their own specific needs.

Coral Reef organisms display adaptations in both physical structure and behavioural life style. All of these adaptations are related to survival – 'to eat, to avoid being eaten and to reproduce' is the law of survival – and all marine creatures involved with coral reefs are continuously fighting their own battles for survival. Physical adaptation and unique behavioural lifestyle can be witnessed with every life form on the reef – and every adaptation is fascinating.

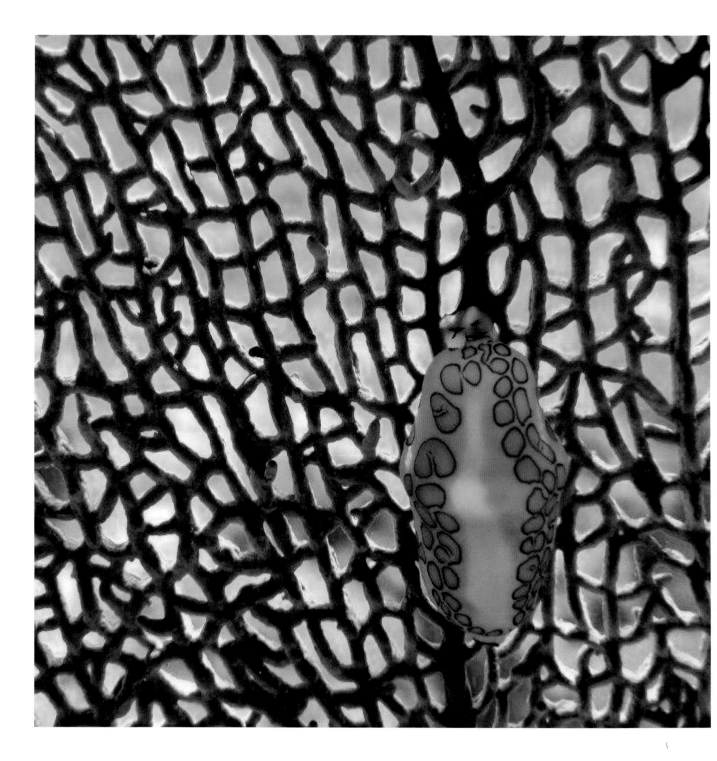

CHAPTER SIX

Spectacular Sea Slugs and Other Strange Critters

There are colourful zooxanthellae algae living within the tissues of numerous coral reef invertebrates such as coral, jellyfish, sponges, giant clams, flatworms, sea slugs and sea squirts. Invertebrates are creatures which have no backbone. All of these organisms are marine invertebrates and the colours endowed by the algae provide a majestic sight within the rich diversity of life on a reef.

Jellyfish

Jellyfish are members of the cnidarian family along with hard and soft corals. Jellyfish have been known in our oceans for 650 million years and scientists have described over 2000 species of jellyfish in our world ocean both large and small. More than 90% of a jellyfish is actually water, as it uses a fluid filled cavity (hydro-skeleton), surrounded by muscles, to change its shape and produce movement.

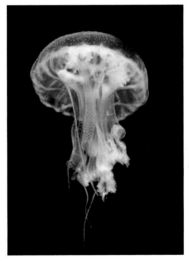

Jellyfish

Jellyfish are not sessile like the corals, but are planktonic as they drift with the currents, although a number of species control their depth with a pulsating swimming motion. Jellyfish feed on phytoplankton, and zooplankton but in turn fall prey to larger marine animals such as turtles.

The largest known jellyfish was washed ashore in Massachusetts, USA in 1870. It had tentacles 36 metres long and a bell diameter of 2 metres across. The tentacles were a glutinous mass formed into eight clumps and from each of these clumps more than 100 tentacles stretched out beneath it. The reddish-brown colour of the tentacles gave it the name of Lion's Mane Jellyfish. It can still be found in the Arctic, the North Atlantic and the North Pacific Oceans.

A mollusc cowrie on a sea fan coral

One fertilized jellyfish egg can produce millions of new jellyfish. However, the *turritopsis nutricula* jellyfish has developed a unique ability to become 'immortal'. Whilst going through the reproductive process it can alter the differentiation stage to a process of 'transdifferentiation' where it can reabsorb itself and turn back into a young polyp. As this process could go on indefinitely, this species of jellyfish could be defined as 'immortal'.

Whilst most jellyfish are harmless to humans, there are some species which carry deadly toxins. A Box Jellyfish has always been known to be particularly nasty, but a discovery in 1964, of a tiny jellyfish called Irukandji has made swimmers nervous. These tiny jellyfish frequent the waters of Northern Australia. The jellyfish injects its venom from threads inside the nemocyst capsules on its tentacles. The results of a sting are incredibly painful, and medical assistance should always be sought during the days after the sting, when the victim suffers with after effects. Without medical attention, some people have died from cardiac arrest.

The best thing to do is to avoid all the areas where Irukandji have been found and take heed of local warnings when swimming.

Sponges

Sponges are among the simplest animals on the planet and it is believed that they evolved from

the first multi-cellular organisms which eventually evolved into animals. They consist of a jelly sandwich– two layers of cells – one either side of a jelly middle layer.

Some species use a silica structure to provide needle like projections which can produce a sting. They are sessile, and draw water into their structures with small hair-like structures, cilia, which by using a waving action to create a current, can draw nutrients

Brighter Yellow Sponge

into the sponge and remove waste products. The water is usually drawn in through the sides of the structure, and leaves through a central chamber.

Coral-eating Sponge - a fierce and particularly nasty predator uses chemical warfare

Sponges are experts at chemical warfare, producing toxins which can kill any other organisms which invade its structure. Sponges are said to be of interest to the pharmaceutical industry as some of the chemical compounds which have been discovered in sponges have anti-cancer and anti-biotic properties. It is estimated that there are over 70% of the estimated 15,000 species of sponges which have yet to be scientifically investigated.

Worms

Worms may not sound very exciting - but marine flatworms are some of the most outstanding organisms in the sea. They can be stunningly colourful, with amazing spots or banded patterns and the rippling movements as they move across coral or through the water make them look like they are dancing. Patterned flatworms have wonderful names e.g. marbled, leopard, and harlequin. Worms have a symbiotic relationships with the algae which gives them their incredible colours.

Flatworms have elementary eyes which can orientate to the intensity and direction of light and flatworms were the first animals to develop bilateral symmetry with a longitudinal axis on one plane, which produces identical halves. All vertebrates have bilateral symmetry – so to find such structures in creatures that evolved so early in the history of life on earth is incredible. Invertebrate flatworms are found in every habitat on earth, and it is believed that there are over 25,000 species.

Flatworm

The flatworms we find in the oceans today are the relatives of possibly the earliest predators on earth dating back to 520 million years ago.

Molluscs

The phylum 'mollusca' contains animals such as bivalves, snails, and cephalopods. Although invertebrates, most of the molluscs have hard parts which they use in shell construction. They are a very successful phylum and have over 130,000 species, mainly snails.

Pharao Cuttlefish

Giant Clams and oysters are bivalves. These creatures like to bury themselves in sediment leaving only their siphon exposed to absorb oxygen and nutrients. Bivalves do not have a head but live inside two hinged shells which have strong muscles attached to them. They can be wonderfully coloured due to the symbiotic relationship they have with algae. They have multiple eyes along the mantle on the inside of their shell and can react to light and shade very quickly. Pointing a camera too close to a giant clam, can create a shadow, which causes the clam to immediately shut.

Cephalopods are also within the phylum of molluscs, with the Nautilus the only remaining creature on Earth from the family *Nautilaceae*, which is related to the ancient ammonites which we now know only as fossils. Nautilus are known as living fossils and have remained unchanged for over 500 million years.

In the same family, the octopus, cuttlefish and squid have all evolved the ability to change colour and skin texture to provide camouflage. They swim backwards using jet propulsion of water through a tube in their mantle.

Octopus and squid have tentacles with suction pads to capture prey, and some have developed an amazing escape trick. They use ink squirted into the water near the eyes of the incoming predator to provide a distraction whilst they escape. The octopus is thought to be the most intelligent member of all the marine invertebrates. The only hard shell they have is their beaked mouths which are incredibly strong. Octopuses mate only once in their life, and by the time juveniles are old enough to look after themselves, both parents have died.

Octopus

Snails and Sea Slugs are members of the class Gastropoda. They have a discrete head and mouth often with a radula which is a serrated feeding organ which can tear and scrape its food from the coral. These creatures are very motile, using a muscular foot to move around the reef. Nudibranchs are sea slugs which do not have an external shell, so their gills are exposed at the rear of the animal. The gills absorb oxygen from the water.

Far Right: Nudibranch

Right: Wart Slug

They are nothing like the slugs we find in our gardens, and these slugs are some of the most beautiful and colourful creatures on earth. Even marine wart slugs can be spectacular.

There is however a price to be paid for such beauty within this phylum. There are also highly poisonous cone snails and textile cones which contain enough toxin to kill a human if they are unlucky enough to stand on one.

Crustaceans

Arthropods are the most successful phylum on Earth with over 1 million species recorded. These organisms evolved first in the marine environment over 300 million years ago, before some species transferred to land and started to evolve into the delightful species of insects that we can find in the terrestrial environment today.

Within the arthropod phylum are the crustaceans. There are over 30,000 species of crustacean, nearly all of which can be found in the marine environment. Crustaceans have a body which is divided into three parts: a head, thorax and abdomen, and a complex exoskeleton composed of chitin. Their outer skeleton is not continuous but formed from sections called somites. They have a number of jointed legs, two pairs of antennae and well-developed claws. Found amongst the marine crustaceans are the tiniest of creatures, the copopods.

Over 1,000 species of shrimps, krill and crabs can be found on the Great Barrier Reef including the amazing Mantis shrimp. This shrimp is famous for having two very formidable hinged claws that fold under its head and then unfurl to create a punch. This 'punch' is the fastest movement known in the marine animal world as the arms unfurl at up to 50 mph, with an acceleration estimated at 10,000 times the force of gravity.

Lobsters and crayfish have incredibly long antennae, which is often the only thing you can see exposed from their hiding place in the crevices of the reef. Both lobsters and shrimps are often nocturnal, they hunt at night. This is a behavioural adaptation which enables them to avoid being predated. After all, these species are not just tasty for humans.

Lobster crabs are the scavengers of the family – they will eat almost anything and coming in many sizes and shapes they often carry other animals on their shells to provide camouflage. Japanese spider crabs hold the record for the largest crab at over 4 metres across. Not a creature to meet up with too often underwater.

Lobster

Echinoderms

These are an ancient group of animals that first roamed the seas about 500 million years ago, and we now have over 6,000 species, all of which live in a marine environment. There are no

Sea Star

terrestrial echinoderms – and the most famous echinoderms are probably the five 'legged' sea stars, although there are some other fascinating species from sea urchins to sea cucumbers.

They have no head, brain or heart and are unique with their radially symmetrically body with a water vascular system. The crinoids can have between 5 to over 200 flexible arms, whilst the brittle stars have the typical five arm symmetry. Sea cucumbers have adapted to lie on one side, and have formed hollow tube legs, whilst sea urchins lay on one side with moveable spines extruding from their body and a set of teeth on their underside used for rasping algae from the reef.

Echinoderms are often toxic, and the Crown of Thorns sea star is an example of a voracious predator, using its toxicity to stun its prey. The sea snail, Triton's Trumpet, is a predator of the Crown of Thorns, but it is popular with collectors of shells, and historically was also used as a horn for seafarers.

Unfortunately, by removing the Triton's Trumpet from the ecosystem in such large numbers, it has enabled the Crown of Thorns to invade, destroy reefs and upset the delicate ecological balance.

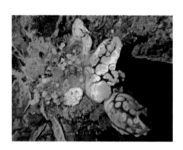

Sea Squirts

Tunicates

Tunicates are sometimes considered to be not true Invertebrates – as they have a primitive 'backbone' called a notochord. They become filter feeders which can either Attach to the reef or drift with the plankton. Sea squirts are Sessile tunicates which can be intensely colourful, from the algae which associate with them, whilst salps are pelagic tunicates which float through the water – sometimes forming chains of up to 20 metres long.

Tunicates can be hermaphrodites or can use the asexual system of reproduction of budding. Some of the amazing adaptations that these creatures have undergone is to develop a heart with two pacemakers, and a brain which produces hormones.

CHAPTER SEVEN

Fantastic Adaptations of Marine Life

Survival

All organisms on the land, in the air, or in the oceans need to eat, they need to avoid being eaten, and they need to reproduce.

In the oceans, however, the environment is particularly harsh as creatures have to absorb their oxygen from the 1% dissolved oxygen present in sea water; regulate their salt intake in saline seas; adapt to water pressure and temperature changes at different depths, as well as dealing with the currents, and waves. Photosynthetic creatures also have to ensure a niche in the environment, where there is enough light for photosynthesis to take place.

Marine organisms exist in a competitive world, constantly being hunted, yet a vast number of species manage to survive and to breed. When we look at the variety of species in the marine environment it is impossible not to be totally amazed at the survival strategies and adaptations that exist. So many creatures are dealing with the struggle for life, in so many different ways.

All of the adaptations we see have evolved from the need to survive and we see Darwin's Theory of Natural Selection working everywhere as we look at ocean life. Marine animals have adapted both physically and behaviourally to cope with the competitiveness of existence in their harsh environment. Some fish have adapted poisonous fins to avoid predators, some come out to feed at night, some fish shoal to provide safety in numbers, whilst others have strange tail or body shape for speed or manoeuvrability. Whatever creature you examine it will have found its own niche of habitat, behaviour and physical adaptation. Some of these adaptations are incredible.

Adaptation

All oxygen breathing animals have had to adapt physiologically to enable them to extract dissolved oxygen efficiently from the water and pass it into their blood. Fish gills are a wonder of adaptation – with the large surface area of gills acting as a powerful gas exchange unit.

Most bony fish living in the top few metres of the sea have developed swim bladders, which act as buoyancy aids and stops them from sinking or floating upwards but fish which live in the deep oceans do not have these large gas spaces, as they would be crushed under the intense pressure.

Research has shown that marine fish absorb seawater through their skin. Some calcium is absorbed but most of the salts are excreted through the gills.

Fish Shape

Differences in fish shape occur depending on the niche in which the creature lives. Flat fish have settled into a niche on the sandy sea bed in shallow seas and bury themselves beneath the sediment.

Flatfish Peacock Flounder

Examples of flat fish are plaice, sole, flounders and turbot – and most of us know them best from their appearance on our plate in a restaurant. Although regularly caught by fishermen, these fish do have a good survival rate.

During their growth and development stage they undergo some of the craziest physical changes witnessed in the animal world. When flatfish are newly hatched, they have a bilateral symmetry a normal 'fishy' shape with a body arranged into two mirrored halves.

The wonderful face of the Peacock Flounder

Within about 30 days after hatching however, compression develops their physical appearance and turns them into a distinctive asymmetrical creature. Firstly, one eye migrates to the other side – so there are two eyes on one side of their body. Their skeletal and digestive tracts alter, they lose one dorsal and one anal fin, their underside turns pale, and their top side becomes camouflaged. Their mouth changes shape and moves to the underside so it can filter invertebrates from the sandy bottom.

Physical adaptations of marine life

Stingrays have a powerful sting in their long tails. Butterfly fish have tiny pointed mouths enabling them to pick out tiny scraps of algae from between the coral, whilst Groupers have large mouths to snap at smaller fish.

Far Left: A Southern Stingray in Grand Turk

Center: Yellowbar Butterfly Fish

Left: Grouper hiding in the coral of the Maldives

Sea urchins protect themselves from most predators by lying face down on the coral and having thick black spines sticking up out of their back. Sea cucumbers, closely related to sea urchins (they are both echinoderms), have developed tubular legs to creep along the sea floor and across the reef.

Far Left: Sea Urchin in Black Sands, Lembeh Straits, Indonesia

Left: Tubular legs of a Sea Cucumber

Trigger fish, however, use a behavioural adaptation to eat the sea urchins as they have developed the ability to shoot a high-powered jet of water at the sea urchin which dislodges it from the coral and enables the trigger fish to turn the urchin over and eat the soft insides.

Lionfish – Red Sea

Lionfish are covered in needle sharp spines across their backs which deliver a poison to any predator, or diver, that gets too close.

Camouflage is an excellent adaptation and used by many marine animals. Cuttlefish are experts at changing colour before your eyes as they move over a coral reef.

67

Chromodorids are wonderfully coloured little sea slugs. They can eat poisonous marine life, and then store the poisons to use on their predators. Their predators are warned off the sea slug because the slug is highly coloured. Bright colours have been adopted by both marine and land animals who want to make sure that their predators do not mistake them for a tasty meal and avoid eating them. There are land animals including poisonous tree frogs, that are usually brightly coloured, and brightly spotted ladybirds which leave a foul taste in a birds' mouth. Once it has eaten one ladybird a bird never wants to eat another so the bright colours warn the predators away from eating them.

Chromodoris – a small nudibranch sea slug

Finally, the physical adaptations developed by creatures of the deep include photo-luminescent organs which can act both as a lure for prey or used as a weapon to escape.

Behavioural adaptations of marine life

Fish such as herring and sardines have adopted shoaling as a behavioural defence. There is definitely safety in numbers and often there are thousands of fish in a shoal. Fish shoals are highly organized as the fish swim parallel to one another and use the fish's lateral line organ to detect the position and movements of its neighbours in the shoal. The line contains sensory cells which register every slight change in the water, and the fish react to each other with rapid coordinated manoeuvres. Although some fish are taken from a shoal, and some predators such as barracuda can sweep through a shoal with a lightning quick attack, the shoaling behaviour does benefit each individual, reducing the likelihood of being eaten.

Shoal of fusiliers

Waiting for their prey to come to them, groupers hide under table corals, moray eels back into crevices, crocodile fish lay motionless on the sand, Jawfish dig a hole in the sea bed and sting rays bury themselves under the sand – all hiding until their prey comes swimming past.

Far Left: Two morays sharing a crevice

Centre: A tiny Jawfish backs into a hole to hide

Left: A Crocodile fish lies in wait

Multiple Survival Strategies

An octopus uses at least three survival strategies – incredible camouflage including a pattern of a false eye which confuses their prey, the ability to hide in crevices, and intelligence.

Frogfish use a lure on their heads, made from a fleshy growth which resembles a fishing rod, it can camouflage itself completely amongst the coral, and it has also adapted its pectoral fins into harder tissue that support the fish when it stands motionless on the coral for a long time. When it opens its mouth, it takes only six milliseconds to capture its prey. The sad part of this wonderful adaptation story is that in concentrating on all these other areas, the frog fish has now 'forgotten' how to swim and moves from rock to rock in a strange wobbly hopping movement.

Stonefish have poisonous spines on their back, but they also bury themselves in the sand. Divers putting a hand on a stonefish are rewarded with severe pain and possible hospitalisation for some days. Some stonefish are even known to allow algae to grow over them.

Poisonous Scorpion fish also remain motionless and are also well camouflaged, so divers have to constantly keep an eye out for them.

Far Left: Frogfish 'standing' in coral

Centre: Stonefish covered in algae

Left: Scorpion fish – highly camouflaged and dangerous

The Blenny Cleaner Mimic employs mimicry to get himself a meal. resembles the Bluestreak Cleaner Wrasse which does a wonderful job of removing old bits of food, parasites or bits of flaking tissue from a larger fish. These large predatory fish do not attempt to eat the wrasse as the fish does such a good job. The little bleeny however, which looks almost identical to the wrasse, jumps in on the act and bites chunks of scale or fin from the larger fish. He uses his look-alike physical features as well as his cheeky behaviour to aid his survival.

Mating Behaviour

Once you have survived then you need to pass on your genes by breeding. Fish mainly use external fertilisation, where a female lays eggs, and a little while afterwards a male fertilise them. Both male and female then leave the eggs to hatch and the newly hatched fish have to fend for themselves. As the chances of survival in this system is lower than that of internal fertilisation (as used by mammals), then the female usually lays thousands of eggs at a time in order that some may survive. One fish, the seahorse, uses the male to incubate the eggs, while a female octopus will mate, lay the eggs and then protect the eggs until they hatch – by which time she is exhausted and has starved herself to death. The male octopus also die after mating. Anemone fish have a family life, however. The anemone family live amongst an anemone coral and are impervious to the stinging cells of the anemone. The parents forcefully protect their young, even attacking large fish or divers who come too close. Trigger fish protect a nest that contains their eggs and can be fearsome in their attacks on other fish as well as divers.

Symbiotic Relationships

Ramoras attach themselves to a turtle shell and feed off the algae, cleaner fish feed on the leftover food in the mouths of moray eels, and gobies living with shrimps are all examples of symbiotic mutualism, where two species help each other to live to the benefit of both species.

Right: Ramoras on Turtle

Far Right: A blue Cleaner Wrasse enters the gill of a Giant Moray Eel

The goby/shrimp relationship is a wonderful example of a symbiotic relationship. A goby is a small reef fish with good eyesight but he needs a burrow so he can hide from predators. The pistol shrimp is a good digger who can keep the burrow clean and tidy, but it has poor eyesight. They share a burrow and the goby protects it by keeping guard as the shrimp works to look after their burrow where they both hide if a predator comes along. Each partner relies on the other for their survival.

Zooanthellae algae live within the tissues of coral and this is known as endosymbiotic mutualism (endo = living inside). Both the algae and the coral benefit from the partnership. The algae gets a place to live without being swept around in the currents, whilst the coral gains the oxygen and glucose produced from photosynthesis in the algae. Both species are happy.

Clown Anemone fish live happily inside the tentacles of anemone coral. Although the coral has stinging cells on the end of its tentacles, the clown fish has adapted its skin to be immune to the poison. The clownfish lays its eggs, and brings up its family within the protection of the anemone, whilst the anemone coral gains protection from being eaten as the clown fish fights off any intruders.

Clownfish living inside the tentacles of an Anemone Coral

It is impossible to describe every form of adaptation used in the marine world. Every diver who visits this strange world has an opportunity to watch fish, or marine invertebrates in their own environment. Every observation records a different animal, using a different survival technique. It is impossible to watch these animals play out their survival strategies and witness the winners and losers in this survival game without an intense feeling of awe and wonder of life in the underwater world.

CHAPTER EIGHT

Scary Sharks & Deadly Dangers

Sharks

The risk of being killed by a shark is about 1 in 3.7 million – and even less if you don't swim in the sea! So why have sharks got this incredibly bad reputation and how much is really known about sharks?

Well, firstly sharks are fish. They have a cartilaginous skeleton which makes them differ from the normal 'bony' fish that everyone knows well. Sharks are incredibly well adapted for their environment as their streamlined bodies allow them to swim with an awesome power through the water with very little effort. They have 5 or 6 gills and rows of replaceable teeth. Although they can only swim forwards, they have excellent control of their buoyancy using a large oily liver to control their depth rather than a gas filled swim bladder. Sharks skin, seen under a microscope, reveals thousands of sharp edges embedded in the skin acting like a suit of armour. Their skin is so rough that in the past the skin of a shark has been used as sandpaper. Sharks have existed for over 350 million years having evolved 100 million years before the dinosaurs.

Left: Juvenile Black Tip Reef Shark – showing its reflection in the crystal clear and shallow waters of the Maldives.

Opposite page: Whale Shark

Sharks in South Africa

Horror films portray sharks as fierce predators that hunt and kill innocent humans, but the truth is much less dangerous, and the chances of a shark attack are extremely low. Sharks are not unpredictable, frenzied killers who search out humans to eat – they actually play an essential part in the marine ecosystem by removing weak and sick animals. Most sharks are not in the least bit dangerous to humans. There are over 370 species of shark, and only five of these have ever been involved with incidents involving humans.

There were some serious incidents in the Red Sea during 2010 with two sharks attacking swimmers. Full investigations were carried out and it was determined that the shark's natural way of life had been 'interfered with by humans' who, it seems, had been feeding the sharks by hand. Hardly surprising then that the sharks were confused when they saw swimmers nearby and mistakenly took them for carrying food. Everyone who enters a strange environment needs to be careful about not disturbing the ecosystem and the natural food webs. In this case, the disturbance of the natural ecosystem caused death and injuries.

Sharks are found in all oceans around the world from the warm waters of the tropics to the cold polar seas. Some live in the deep dark waters of the ocean, whilst others bask in sunlit waters close to the surface. A few sharks swim up rivers and sometimes are found in fresh water lakes.

Although usually all have streamlined bodies there are many different shapes, sizes and colours of shark. Sharks that live on the sea bed have long eel-like flattened bodies whilst the sharks that swim long distances through oceans have a more rounded shape. Those which live in open seas have to move continuously through the water to enable water to cross their gills and help them to breathe, although some sharks are found sitting in crevices on coral reefs allowing the current to drift through their mouths, and some sharks can use their gill muscles to actively pump water across their gills.

Sharks don't have ears with flaps, but they do have tiny openings at the top of their head which allow sharks to respond quickly to sounds. Sharks listen for sounds of injured fish as they flail in the water. A shark also has an excellent sense of smell. Recent research has found that just 10 drops of tuna juice in a full-size swimming pool can attract a shark in seconds.

Shark eyes are similar to human eyes, containing rods, cones, cornea, iris, pupils, lens and retina and it is believed that sharks can distinguish colour. Their night vision is better than humans as their eyes have increased light-sensitivity and they can see in the dark up to 10 times better than we can. Sharks rotate their eyes for protection when feeding and some sharks also have a membrane which acts as a moveable shield across their eyes. Their eyesight is not perfect, however.

Tiger sharks, for instance, love to eat turtles but seen from the deep when the sea turtle is on the surface, a shark can mistake a surf board and surfer for its favourite crunchy turtle snack. Sharks are also lured into the mistake of taking a chunk of human by mistake when humans are swimming in shallow water. The splashing created by a human swimmer apparently resembles an injured animal which the shark sees as an easy meal. Sharks don't choose to eat humans, and such shark attacks are just a mistake.

A very special adaptation of sharks is their use of electro-location. The dark spots on the shark's snout and lower jaw are specialised pores containing jelly-filled canals that allow the shark to pick up weak electrical signals. This very different 'sixth' sense allows a shark to sense direction and to help it find its food.

Sharks are not always feeding. They eat only 25% their own body weight every 2 or 3 days and not all sharks have ferocious teeth for hunting humans and tearing them to shreds. Sharks can have between 12,000 to 30,000 teeth during its lifetime. These teeth are attached to the mouth in a type of conveyor belt, with the shark losing the teeth every time they take in a big bite of food. Different sharks have different teeth depending on the food they eat – strong teeth can munch away at crabs, serrated teeth can tear flesh, smooth teeth can cope with most fish – but there are a number of species of shark which only eat plankton 87. Sharks in South Africa and krill. Whale sharks are the largest of all sharks, reaching up to 18m long, yet they filter the sea as they swim, circulating water at up to 2 litres per second. Basking sharks are seen around many shores during the summer taking their fill of plankton and krill. Basking sharks are believed to have been the inspiration of many sea monster tales, especially when grouped together at the surface yet far from being a sea monster they are the gentlest of creatures.

Many sharks are curious about humans. Hammerheads are the latest in the evolutionary line of sharks and are not known to harm humans. They feed at night, hunting alone, eating small invertebrates which they filter from the sand. Their mouths are flat and positioned under their head. Hammerheads are known for their intelligence and they gather in social groups during the day often coming up to divers to 'have a look' at them, then swimming peacefully away.

Oceanic white tips sharks are well known to divers, who watch in amazement as they swim effortlessly and gracefully through water, often attended by pilot fish who wait for scraps from the shark's meal, or who eat the parasites off the shark's body.

Oceanic White Tip Shark - Red Sea

Watching these creatures in the sea is no more dangerous than watching lions on a safari in Africa you just need to be aware of their power. By acting sensibly divers will get the sight of a lifetime if they remain still in the water as this large and impressive predator swims past, giving a majestic, awesome and a stunning view of one of the strongest creatures in the oceans.

Deadly Dangers in the Ocean

So - if sharks are mainly 'cuddly and harmless' – what should humans be careful of when swimming in our fantastic oceans? Well, there are creatures that bite, and creatures that sting, and some that use deadly poisons.

Creatures that Bite

Moray Eels have a reputation for having a decent bite – but they rarely attack a human. A bite from a moray is usually the mistake of the diver for putting their hand too close to the moray. Morays live in crevices in coral reefs, and they can be aggressive if you get too close. To the moray a quick snap at a possible predator is a measure to protect their survival.

Moray Eel hiding in a crevice

Titan Trigger fish are well known for being dangerous to humans if disturbed during the nesting season. Male Triggerfish can grow up to 23 cm in length, are very powerful and have enormous teeth. The males look after the nest and are forceful in ensuring that humans, or any other

creatures don't get too close. Triggerfish have been known to bite through thick rubber fins as well as to bite a diver through their wetsuit. Serious injuries have been recorded, and it is a very scary encounter for any diver who experiences an attack.

Small fish, such as damselfish and anemone fish protect their nests, and their young by aggressive behaviour towards predators, or even a diver, or snorkeler. They rush out at speed and can even hit a diver's mask. This certainly has the desired effect of making the humans keep their distance.

Far Left: Titan Triggerfish

Creatures that use Poisons

Most jelly fish species are harmless, but some have a deadly reputation. Box jellyfish, named for their shape, have tentacles extending from each corner of their bodies. The jellies can inflict a fatal sting containing a neurotoxin, and without an anti-venom death occurs very quickly as it stops the heart from beating.

Although one of the smallest of the octopus family at about 10 cm long, a blue-ringed octopus can pack a deadly bite and its poison can kill a human in seconds. When under attack the octopus produces an electric blue glow around itself and injects its poison through a bite from its beak like mouth. There is no antidote to its poison, and death of the victim occurs quickly. So, beware! Check your travel information, and if you want to go rock pooling in the Pacific then take heed of local warnings in order to ensure you and your family's safety.

Creatures from the ray family, Manta Rays, Eagle Rays and Blue Spotted rays are shy, harmless and gentle creatures that are beautiful to watch as they move effortlessly through the water, but stingrays have a spine on their tail which can inject a poison that causes pain, swelling and muscle cramps. If the poison enters the body near the heart, then a swimmer can die from muscular paralysis.

It is totally the swimmer's fault if they get stung by a hydra or anemones as these animals are sessile - and do not chase the swimmer. Brushing up against them can produce a sting which causes a rash and sometimes hospitalisation but, although incredibly painful, is unlikely to be fatal.

Some sea snails can inject a neurotoxin from harpoon-like teeth if stood on, on the sandy sea bottom. Cone snails are one of the most venomous creatures on earth, and paralysis of the victim occurs rapidly. These snails also use a wonderful camouflage system, so it is difficult to see them in the sand.

Venomous Fish

Lionfish, scorpion fish and stonefish are all venomous fish that inflict their poisons through spines on their back. Lionfish are quite open about their protective system as they swim through the seas proudly displaying their poisonous spines for everyone to see and avoid.

Stonefish and scorpion fish however try to hide or disguise themselves. Stonefish are sand coloured fish and they bury themselves in the seabed with just their eyes and their spines visible, whilst scorpion fish are the masters of camouflage and are very difficult to distinguish amongst the coral and invertebrates as they move around a reef. Puffer fish are relatively harmless in the water, but chefs have to ensure that they remove a deadly poisonous part of the fish before serving it in a restaurant as a speciality.

Deadly Reptiles

Sea Snakes normally take no notice of humans, but they are territorial animals and will attack if they feel threatened or if you invade their 'space'. If swimming in tropical waters where these reptiles make their home, then as with sharks, treat them with respect and be wary of their presence.

Sea Snake

Always take advice from the local community about where to swim and what not to do. Divers are always advised to take care of the marine environment and to avoid conflict with the seas natural inhabitants – 'take only photographs and leave only bubbles' – is a wonderful philosophy and divers must do all they can to preserve the survival of some of the most amazing creatures on earth.

CHAPTER NINE

There's Not Just Fish in the Sea

Marine Mammals

The majority of mammals are land based, but whether they are land or marine mammals they are identified as being hairy, giving birth to live young, suckling their young and having mammary glands – from which they get their name. Many species of marine mammal spend all of their lives in the water but whether they live partially on land fully or in the sea, they are all reliant on their food from the oceans. Marine mammals are a diverse group of roughly 120 species within three main orders of classification, Cetaceans – the whales and dolphins, Sirenians – manatee and dugong, and Carnivora – the otters, seals, walrus and polar bears.

Most marine animals, such as fish, extract oxygen from water using adapted gills, but marine mammals which live wholly in water use blowholes, whilst polar bears and otters have lungs like land mammals. Blubber of marine mammals varies from 5 cm thick in small whales and seals, to over 30 cm thick in large whales.

Cetaceans, the whales and dolphins and Silurians, the manatee family, have no hair but the Carnivora have thick layers of fur which helps to insulate the animal but can contribute to drag when swimming, slowing the animal down and giving it a disadvantage. A balance has to be sought between being a slow swimmer and being cold. Obviously, evolution of fur has been a successful adaptation for animals which reside in the higher latitudes, such as polar bears and seals.

Other adaptations that aid marine mammals in retention of body heat are high internal body temperature, blubber, hair, and a counter-current exchange system in fins when the heat contained in the blood flow is exchanged between closely positioned blood vessels. Behavioural adaptation such as seals and walrus hauling themselves out of the cold water and grouping together, helps to retain warmth in cold climates.

Carnivora

The marine mammals in the order Carnivora are more closely related to terrestrial carnivores such as bears and weasels than they are to whales or dolphins.

Polar Bears

Polar Bears are competent swimmers, but they are the least adapted for a full marine life. They rest, mate, give birth and suckle their young on land but they can only survive by obtaining their food from the sea.

Although classed as a marine animal, the Polar Bear is also the largest land predator with males reaching heights of 2.6m and weighing up to 900 lbs. A female can reach 2m in height and weigh up to 500 lbs. They are the top predator in the Arctic. Polar Bears are only found in the northern region of our planet, the Arctic, where the temperature ranges from -34°C in the winter to 0°C in the summer – which explains the incredible adaptations a polar bear has for surviving the cold. Its system of thermal regulation has both physical and behavioural components. The skin is black which allows it to pick up as much heat from the Sun as possible, and there is a high thermal conductivity in the fur in both air and water. The fur, fat and sub-dermal blood supply are specialised and blood vessels can change direction of blood flow to retain heat. The pads on a polar bear's feet are covered in hair and this adds another layer of insulation between the bear's foot and the ice or snow. It also reduces the problem of walking on slippery ice. The bear also uses postural and behaviour mechanisms during extreme climate conditions.

Polar Bear without any snow or ice - a look into the future?

Polar bears spend a lot of time moving great distances in search of food. They can range between 20,000 to 135,000 square miles per year. They can swim over 45 miles in a day, at a steady rate of 6mph, and have been observed in the seawater 50 miles from ice or land. They swim with a doggie paddle motion with their head and some of their back above water, whilst their blubber helps to keep them afloat.

Polar bears do not drink water, as they get all the water they need from the animals they eat. The bears have a predator jaw with huge canine teeth and a line of large carnassial teeth which they use to break bones. The main diet of a polar bear is seal, although they will eat anything from eggs to walrus if they are hungry. The bears will sniff out a seal hole, then use its front paws to smash through the ice. It uses its claws to hook out the seal. They are adapted to a 'feast and famine' feeding regime where they can eat a large amount of food when it is available, and then starve for a length of time, until the next meal becomes available. The bears can also alter their metabolism and go into a form of hibernation at any time during storms, both in summer or winter. They can live in dens of snow and ice for 48 months with no food, no urination and no defaecation. Polar Bears are one of the most highly adapted creatures on earth for living in a hostile environment.

Classed as an endangered species, Polar bears are now estimated to number around 25,000 bears. Global warming is destroying their habitat, with the major problems occurring being a decrease in area, duration and thickness of the ice floes which stops the polar bear hunting for seals. As the conditions required for the building of the snow birthing dens are declining, female bears are unable to protect bear cubs from the harsh conditions, and once the young bears are out of the den and learning to hunt, then starvation affects cub survival rates.

If polar bears were to become extinct due to loss of ice in the Arctic then their niche would most likely be filled by Orcas – the largest of the dolphin family, who do not have a significant presence in the Arctic at present, but if ice were to disperse, then the opening of the sea area would allow the Orcas to become the top predator in the Arctic.

Sea Otters

A Sea Otter is a competent swimmer – it is the heaviest member of the weasel family and they find their food from the sea and rest, mate, give birth and suckle in the water. They can grow up to 1.2 metres long, weigh 20 kgs and live up to 10-15 years. They also have the claim to fame of being the smelliest of all mammals.

Otters eat clams, mussels, sea snails and sea urchins and use small rocks or other objects as tools to open shellfish. Their hind legs are well adapted for a life in the sea, with webbed back feet, clawed front paws for opening claim shells and they can dive up to 100m to collect their food.

Although their bodies lack blubber, they have the densest fur amongst all mammals with 250,000 to a million hairs per square inch. Often found in kelp forests in areas off the Californian coast it is estimated there are 150,000 otters spread across Scotland, North America, Alaska and Russia.

Seal - off Lundy Island, UK

True Seals and Eared Seals

There are 20 species of true seals, 16 species of eared seals, more commonly known as sealions, and just one species of walrus.

True Seals crawl on their bellies and use their small front flippers to pull themselves over the ice. Eared seals walk on

81

their adapted flippers and also can be recognised by a conspicuous ear flap. Seals can dive for up to 25 minutes to depths of over 180m. They close down their metabolic system by slowing their heart rate as they enter the water. Some seals have been known to dive to 250 m.

Seals may live for up to 30 years, and feed on fish, shrimp, crabs and squid. They don't chew their food but swallow it whole just crushing the shells of crustaceans with carnassial teeth at the rear of their jaw. Seals are hunted by orcas, polar bears and humans.

Elephant seals are a species of eared seal that can range up to 6m in height and they have a strange 'trunk' which can be inflated. They are able to dive to incredible depths up to 1,500m for up to 2 hours at a time due to a flexible ribcage which allows their lungs to compress, thus dealing with the increased water pressure. Elephant seals exhibit fierce fighting skills when living in large groups on the land. Once an endangered species, elephant seals are now legally protected and have recovered from the brink of extinction.

Although aggressive when mating, walrus are sociable animals, living in large groups in the Arctic Circle. They have two large tusks and can do the 'tooth walk' to help pull themselves across ice. Their snouts have incredibly sensitive whiskers which help them to find crabs in the seabed. Walrus hunting by humans in the 18th and 19th centuries reduced the numbers, and now it is only legal for native Alaskans to hunt these fascinating creatures.

Sirenians

There are two types of Sirenian – Manatees and Dugongs. Sirenians are more closely related to elephants than to marine mammals such as whales or dolphins. There are three species of manatee, the West Indian manatee in the Caribbean, the West African and the Amazonian manatee. There is just one species of Dugong. These animals are totally aquatic and only differ in tail and mouth shape and length of flipper. Their brains are very smooth with only a few surface folds, and as these folds are associated with intelligence, it is likely that these creatures are a little slow witted. They are found in shallow waters and are gentle and slow-moving herbivores. Their slow reproductive rate has brought them to the edge of extinction, and they are also finding living alongside humans to be difficult as they need to surface every 35 minutes from the shallow water. They are now endangered due to collisions with boats, and entanglement in fishing lines.

Dugong

Cetaceans
Various species of whales, dolphins, porpoises and narwhales belong to the order Cetacean.

Whales
There are two types of whales – toothed whales and baleen whales. Baleen whales are krill and plankton eaters that feed through a baleen sheet that hangs from the top jaw and filters small animals and plankton from the water. Baleen is a keratin substance (similar to the substance in humans which makes hair and fingernails). The baleen whales are the larger of the two suborders of whale and have grown so large that they cannot chase after enough food quickly enough to supply their needs, so they just swim through the water and filter their food all day long, breathing through two blowholes. Blue, Grey and Humpback Whales feast in Arctic waters in the spring when krill is the most abundant.

Blue Whales are the largest animal on the planet. They can live up to 90 years, measure up to 30 metres, weigh up to 200 tonnes, with their tongues alone weighing as much as an elephant, and with hearts as big as a car. Blue Whales can consume 4 tons of krill in a day, feeding whilst they travel hundreds of miles a day using sonar navigation. They are the loudest animals on earth and can hear each other up to 1000 miles apart.

There are 65 species of Toothed whales including Sperm, Pilot and Beluga Whales, Orca (Killer Whale), Dolphins and Porpoises. They all have one blowhole and are all successful predators. Using oxygen from their muscles, as well as from their blood, this enables them to hunt at extreme depths for long periods of time. They use echo-location at depth in the dark to find their food and swallow their food whole. Sperm Whales can dive to at least 1000m where pressure is 100 times that of the surface.

The Orca is a member of the dolphin family. It is a very efficient predator and even kills baby Blue Whales. The only enemy of an Orca is a human being. Narwhales are members of the porpoise family. They have one long ivory tusk which grows through the upper lip, thought to be used in a mating ritual.

Dolphins are probably one of our favourite marine mammals, with documented reports of dolphins having interaction with humans, including helping injured humans to safety. They are certainly intelligent, inquisitive, curious and playful. Dolphins have a long gestation period of up to 18 months, before they give birth to their offspring and the young dolphins stay with their mothers until they are five years old learning the skills of hunting. Dolphins have a complicated communication system of whistles and clicks but no humans have yet been able to understand their messages.

Marine Reptiles

Marine Iguanas

Marine iguanas are land-based lizards that rely on the ocean for their food - marine algae, growing on the rocks in shallow seas. They are cold-blooded creatures so need to bask in the Sun in the morning to warm up their blood enough to allow them to move. Their dark skin allows them to quickly absorb the radiation from the Sun, raising their temperature to 36°C. Once warm, they slip into the seawater and dive down to the rocks to eat the algae. They use their powerful tails to push them through the water and use their clawed front legs to grab the algae out of the crevices. When they return to the surface, they will have cooled down due to the lower water temperature of 10°C, so again they

stand in the Sun to warm up. They use a nasal gland to excrete salt, so they continuously sneeze, leaving them with a white salt-encrusted nose. As these iguanas stand around most of the day trying to keep warm it makes them easy prey for hawks, owls, and snakes. They are endemic to the Galapagos Islands, and are considered to be facing a high risk of extinction.

Far Right: Marine Iguana

Turtles

Turtles have been on our planet for 200 million years and there are seven species of marine turtle in the world ocean. Turtles can live for decades and can even live for up to a year without food. Green turtles can dive for up to five hours before surfacing to breathe, hold high levels of carbon dioxide in their blood, and swim up to 35 mph to escape danger. Some turtles seem oblivious to poisons and stings and can feast on toxic sea sponges without being harmed. Salt is excreted through a turtle's eyes, producing moisture which resembles tears.

Hawksbill Turtles spend most of their year feeding off the South American coast, but females travel more than 200 km to lay eggs on Ascension Island. This migration pattern is one of many in which all the different species of sea turtles are involved. Adult females return to the beach where they were born to lay their eggs in the sand. A male turtle, however, will probably never leave the sea to return to land. The gender of a turtle is dependent on the temperature at which the egg is incubated, with the higher the temperature in the nest, the more females being born. Hatchlings, barely 15 cm long, take a high risk run to the sea, across the hot sand and are then carried away by the waves and currents. It is estimated that only one out of a thousand sea turtles survive the hatching and their early sea life.

The migration pattern of turtles is still being studied but we do know that they travel thousands of miles from breeding grounds to feeding grounds every year. The leatherback turtle is recorded as the largest sea turtle, reaching lengths of over 1.8 metres and weighing up to 360kg Leatherback turtles also hold the record for the longest journey through the ocean. In 2008 a female turtle was tagged and tracked by satellite for over 12,000 miles, travelling across the Pacific and back again. Leatherback turtles are found in warm seas across the world's oceans.

Sea Snakes

Commonly found in the Indian and Pacific oceans, sea snakes are all members of the cobra species. They live in the sea, but surface to breathe every hour. This restricts the depths to which they can dive so they are found mainly in shallow seas. Nearly 50 species of sea snake have been identified and they are all poisonous, using a bite to pass venom into their victims. Growing to only 2 metres long they swim into crevices hoping to trap small fish, bite their victim and then withdraw until the poison has done its job. Then, they pop back into the crevice and retrieve their meal. Sea kraits tend to ignore divers but have been caught up in fishing nets, sometimes biting the fishermen as they try to release the snake. Death from a sea snake bite can occur in minutes.

Seabirds - Albatross

Although born on land, the albatross is famous as the seabird which spends its life soaring above the sea. The albatross has the largest wingspan of all birds at 11 feet and can glide effortlessly in the winds over the oceans, without even a flap of its wings.

Albatross depend entirely on the oceans for their food, preferring shoaling fish or squid, and are just occasionally seen floating on the surface of the sea as it finishes a meal. They touch down for short periods in their life on remote islands to breed, and researchers believe that breeding couples may mate for life. Forming large breeding colonies, they produce just one egg, but take great care of the offspring as it grows. When nearly ten months old the young fly the nest and then take nearly ten years to reach sexual maturity and return to their island to breed for themselves. Albatross have been known to live for over 50 years, and 21 species have been identified. Albatross are threatened with extinction due to feral rats attacking their eggs, pollution in the ocean, and the dangers of longline fishing where Albatross see the bait on the fishing lines, become hooked on the lines and drown.

Penguins

It has been thought that humans love penguins so much because of their comical human style of upright walking and this may be correct, but penguins are highly adapted for their survival and they can be admired for their ability to survive in some of the most hostile conditions on earth and for being wonderful parents.

Penguins first arrived on Earth about 40 million years ago. There are now 18 recognised species and they can be found mainly in the southern hemisphere, although one species inhabits the Galapagos Islands which are on the equator. The largest species, Emperor penguins, live on ice in the Antarctic and enter very cold water to catch their food. Penguins are insulated by layers of blubber beneath their skin and tightly packed feathers on their skin, which trap air.

Penguins are birds that cannot fly but they are incredibly good at diving and swimming. They have streamlined bodies and can swim at speeds up to 15 mph, being able to turn quickly in the water to chase their food and avoid predators. Their 'wings' may not allow them to fly, but they are perfectly adapted for swimming and their tail and feet can act as rudders. They can hold their breath for up to 20 minutes under water.

Penguins feed on fish, squid and krill. They have a hook in their bill and backward facing bristles on their tongues to hold onto their catch as they swim through the water. There is a gland near their beak which filters out the salt.

Penguins mate for life and make excellent parents with male penguins incubating the eggs on top of their leathery feet and beneath a feathered belly flap, for many months of the year in the most extreme of weather conditions. The male penguins use a group strategy for survival during the winter which enables the eggs to survive.

"You don't have to hide your head pal, just stand still like me and smile"

Highly sociable animals, they live in large rookeries, and it is believed that penguins mostly communicate through body language, by movements of their head and flippers although Rockhopper penguins also use loud calls.

Penguin survival is threatened by water pollution with oil spills being particularly hazardous to their survival. They have natural predators, the giant petrels and some species of seal, but they are a very successful species with an estimated population of 100 million worldwide.

CHAPTER TEN

The Magic of Seawater

Water is a 'magical' substance. It is the only substance on earth that can be found naturally in the three 'states of matter' – solid, liquid and gas. As a solid it is ice, as a liquid it is water, and as a gas it is steam. Water (70%) and ice (10%) on Earth covers 80% of the Earth's surface.

Water is made of two hydrogen molecules and one oxygen molecule – making H_2O. Hydrogen and oxygen by themselves, of course, are gases not liquids. Gases are invisible – they are very small atoms and they love to spread out but when water is formed – one billion, billion molecules form a pinhead size droplet to become the most common substance on Earth.

So how can two gases combine to form this 'magical' substance? Oxygen is a very friendly atom – it has an affinity to join other elements easily and to become a compound. When one oxygen atom joins with two hydrogen atoms, they share four tiny negatively charged particles called electrons. These electrons make the H_2O molecule stay in shape, but they give a slight imbalance in the electrical charge within the molecule. The result is that water molecules are drawn together and join by weak forces called hydrogen bonds.

Water is a solvent – a substance in which another substance can dissolve – and the charged particles of water attract the charged particles that make up salt. Hard or soft water depends on the quantity of 'salts' dissolved into the water. In the United Kingdom, the famous White Cliffs of Dover, for example, are made from the 'salt' calcium carbonate, which comes from the shells and skeletons of decomposing sea creatures under the ocean where the cliffs first formed as a sedimentary rock. The water that trickles through the rocks into the ground water beneath the cliffs is very hard water as it contains so much of the dissolved calcium carbonate from the surrounding rocks.

Surface tension and heat capacity

Water has some very special properties such as high surface tension and high heat capacity. High surface tension is formed when the water molecules join together to form a 'skin' created by the electrical forces in the molecule. The molecules are attracted to each other and the bonds are quite difficult to break – thus creating the skin effect. Creatures like pond skaters are adept at walking on water – their trick is to spread out their long legs and support their lightweight bodies with long legs which doesn't put too much weight on the water and doesn't break the 'skin'.

Water moves through plants from roots to leaves when water is absorbed from the soil by the roots. The water is transported upwards through the plant by special tubes, and the water 'climbs' up the stem – using the stickiness of water tension.

Surface tension also helps to form waves, as the water droplets stick together and create a flow of water. Then, as a wave breaks, the energy is released The wave edges turn firstly into spray and then into water vapour, eventually turning into the invisible individual atoms of oxygen and hydrogen gas.

High heat capacity is a very important property of water. Heat capacity is the quantity of heat required to raise the temperature by 1°C. Water in the oceans has a higher specific heat capacity than on land, so when the Sun is shining, the oceans take longer than land to heat up. However, once warmed, the oceans retain their heat longer than a land mass. Oceans, because of their enormous coverage of the Earth's surface, are a vast store of energy and although the Sun constantly shines on the oceans, the temperature changes very little.

The oceans maintain the stability of our climates around the world due to high heat capacity of seawater. Oceans absorb solar energy and move the heat energy around the world in surface currents. The Gulf Stream brings warm currents to the UK, and without its warmth, the UK would have the same cold conditions found in Canada during the winter. By contrast to snowy, cold Canada, there are palm trees which grow on the mild west coast of Scotland, due entirely to the warmth from the Gulf Stream. Around the world the currents in the oceans control water temperatures. The Galapagos Islands actually lie on the equator, and the water surrounding them would be expected to be warm, but the sea around the islands is so cold that a species of penguins happily lives in that area. The cold water is due to cold currents being circulated in the area from the north and from the cold Peru Current from the south.

What is in sea water?

The world's oceans contain approximately 1.35 billion cubic kilometres of sea water and dissolved in the water are 45 million billion tons of salts, gases and other substances. There is an extraordinary mixture of minerals and liquid that make up sea water, 96% of sea water is water, whilst 3% is salts. The remaining 1% is made up of small amounts of substances such as dissolved organic and inorganic materials, particulates and of course – dissolved atmospheric gases. The gas content of the ocean depends on the temperature and salinity of the ocean. The gas content of the ocean differs vastly from the gas content of the atmosphere with over a hundred times more oxygen atoms in the atmosphere than in the ocean.

GAS	ATMOSPHERE	OCEAN
Nitrogen	79%	10-20 ppm/l
Oxygen	23%	0-5 ppm/l
Carbon Dioxide	0.03%	65-110 ppm/l
Other Gases (Argon, Krypton)	0.97%	0-020 ppm/l

(*ppm/l = parts per millilitre of liquid)
Gas content of the Ocean

Oxygen is absorbed into the ocean by diffusion from the atmosphere and is also produced by the photosynthesis of phytoplankton and algae.

Carbon Dioxide is very soluble in water, and sea water holds more CO_2 than any other gas. The CO_2 combines chemically with H_2O to form a weak carbonic acid, H_2CO_3, which leads to the ocean, overall, being slightly alkaline. The carbon dioxide is quickly used up in photosynthesis by phytoplankton, and it is this process which produces the gas oxygen plus the substance glucose which is a food source for life in the oceans. Carbon dioxide is also taken up by organisms and used to form their skeletons and shells. When these creatures die, they sink to the bottom of the ocean and the carbon dioxide becomes embedded into sedimentary rock – taking millions of years to move back to the surface where the CO_2 is released slowly. Carbon dioxide is absorbed quickly from the atmosphere but gets released slowly – so the oceans are considered to be a carbon sink for the excess carbon dioxide which is being produced around the world as part of global warming.

Why is the sea salty?

If one litre of seawater is evaporated, then 35 grams of salts would be obtained. Out of 35 grams, 27 grams would be sodium chloride – common salt. The remaining salts are compounds of sulphate, magnesium, calcium and potassium. These salts have come from the weathering of continents, with rivers bringing the salts into the oceans. As the Earth formed there was outgassing from volcanoes and even today gases and salts are spewed out from hydrothermal vents and volcanoes under the sea. The salts are recycled around the planet, with dissolved salts being removed from seawater to form new minerals at the seabed before taking millions of years to form into rock at the surface and then be weathered down again. The salt content of the oceans is in a steady state, with the same salt content being present for many hundreds of millions of years. Calcium carbonate is an important salt which forms the sedimentary rock, limestone. It is limestone sedimentary rock which contains most of the early fossil remains and has given us so much information about the development of life on Earth.

Drinking water

Water is an essential element to life on Earth – but 97% of all water on earth is saline and undrinkable. Out of the 3% fresh water on Earth – 2% is locked up in ice in the Antarctic – so fresh drinking water is a valuable commodity. Removing salt from water to provide safe drinking water (desalination) is expensive and highly technical – but worth every penny to countries where water is scarce. In 2020 only 71% of the human population had access to a clean water supply.

Minerals in the Sea

Most ocean minerals are insoluble – they don't dissolve in the water. Quartz is the most common mineral form of silicon dioxide – it forms most of the sand and sandstone which is found both in sedimentary rock formed under the sea, but also at the boundaries between ocean and continents. There have been over 80 trace elements identified in sea water – one of which is gold and it is said that there is more gold in a ton of sea water than in a ton of gold ore. The problem is that it is incredibly difficult to extract. Sea water is, however, a rich source of some commercially important chemical elements – such as bromine and magnesium.

Human effects on the Chemistry of the Oceans

Humans have had an effect in recent years on the oceans, as well as on the atmosphere of our planet. We use the oceans as a dump for sewage and industrial waste, we have had catastrophic oil spillages, and marine litter is a major cause for concern. Although the oceans allow for fast dilution of many harmful substances, not all substances are soluble. The oceans now carry trace metals, bacteria, viruses, and poisons which can have a long life in the ocean environment.

The dumping of sewage can cause vast areas of seabed to be barren and unable to support life and these areas can stretch many kilometres from the outfall pipes near the shore. Unfortunately, because it is underwater – it is unseen, and few people understand the damage which is being done to the ocean environment.

It is estimated that over seven million pieces of litter enter the marine ecosystem per day – the majority of the objects which are found are made of plastic which has not been able to decompose in the water. Poor disposal of fishing nets can cause harm to wildlife, especially turtles, dolphins and larger mammals.

CHAPTER ELEVEN
The Interesting Bits of Ocean Physics

Temperature in the Oceans

Heat is transferred from the Sun to the Earth in vast quantities. Around the equator and mid-latitudes, it is estimated that over 10 million billion calories of heat are transferred from the atmosphere to the ocean every second. That is likely to be more than a million times the power consumed by the whole world's population at the same time. All of this movement of heat has an amazing effect on the climate and weather on Earth.

The ocean has different temperatures according to the depth at which it is measured. At the surface the temperature ranges between 8°C and 30°C, depending on the degree of solar heating. Water down to 1,000 metres is more constant, ranging from 8°C to 10°C, and this area of water will have thermoclines – where the change in the temperature of the water can be felt as depth increases. The sea floor is constant at 2°C but polar oceans record water temperatures at 0°C and the water is constantly cold.

Water Pressure

Scientists measure pressure in bars. At sea level the measurement is 1 bar, but the pressure increases 1 bar for every 10 metres of depth due to the weight of the water above. At 10 metres there is 2 bar of pressure, whilst at 40 metres it is 5 bar. Human divers have to be very careful as they descend, and even more importantly, they have to follow the rules of ascent carefully to avoid build-up of nitrogen in their blood and consequent decompression sickness. When diving at depths below 30m divers can start to develop nitrogen narcosis which causes an inability to think and concentrate, and a diver is prone to time loss which can be a major cause of diving accidents.

The Sky and the Sea

A glass of seawater is transparent – so what makes the sea seem blue on a warm sunny day? To answer this question, we firstly have to understand that our light comes from the Sun, it travels in straight lines, and that white light is made up of colours, which have different wavelengths.

The way to remember the colours which make up white light is to use a mnemonic such as 'Roy G Biv' – or 'Richard of York Gave Battle in Vain' – which helps to remember the colours in the correct order – Red, Orange, Yellow, Green, Blue, Indigo and Violet. All light travels in a straight line but as light travels from the Sun through the atmosphere of the Earth, then the particles in the air start to get in the way, and the light gets scattered known as refraction. Refraction means that the light waves change direction as they hit the molecules or dust particles in the air. When short wavelengths of light hit small objects, they scatter more than light with a longer wavelength. Red light has the longest wavelength of light, and blue (together with indigo and violet) has the shortest wavelengths of light. So, when sunlight hits a small particle in the atmosphere it is the blue light which scatters first – leaving the other colours to continue to travel to the surface of the Earth. The result is that all the scattering of the blue light creates a blue atmosphere – which of course is our 'blue sky'.

Not all the blue light scatters by hitting particles in the sky – some blue light is still in the sunlight which hits the sea – but the same thing occurs when the light hits the sea – the shorter wavelength of the blue light gets scattered first when the light reaches the sea – so the water looks blue from the refracted blue light. There is of course a second reason for the sea to look blue – the sea reflects the blue of the sky. It is noticeable that when the sky is cloudy and overcast – then the sea doesn't look so blue. So, the answer to 'why is the sea blue?' can be found in the physics of refraction and reflection of light.

Some sea water in the world is always clear – and you can see to the seabed beneath a boat – but this only occurs where the water is still, calm and unpolluted. The sea can sometimes look like brown or green soup, even when the sun is shining, and this is due to the number of particles being moved about in the water. If the movement of the water above the seabed is rough, then the sand and grit particles on the seabed create a 'dirty' sea.

An example, as the whole of the North Sea moves down from Norway towards the Straights of Dover in the UK, the sea tries to move through the smallest width of the English Channel between England and France and the sea becomes choppy as the waves become confused. The choppy sea then disturbs the sand particles on the seabed which turns the sea into a yellow/green mixture of liquid and particles.

So 'why are clouds white?' or 'why does the Sun look red at night?' The cloud question has a quick answer – the particles of water in the clouds present a larger object than the dust and smaller particles which refracted the blue light out of the atmosphere – and if the particles are large then the longer light wavelengths will also be refracted. Water droplets in clouds are so large that they reflect all the colours from the long wavelengths of red right through to the short wavelengths of blue and the light is not split into its separate colours. So, the clouds are white because they contain all the colours, which then make white light.

Sunset in Florida, USA

The Sun goes red at sunset because the light is travelling through more air due to the angle of the Sun through the atmosphere. The more air the light has to travel through, then the more particles it will meet, and the more the light wavelengths will scatter. By the time the Sun has reached a low point in the sky at sunset – the only colour left is the longest wavelength – red as all the other colours have been refracted. Compare the two photographs of a Florida sunset above. In the image on the left the sky is red, orange, and bright yellow. These colours in white light have longer wavelengths than green, blue, indigo or violet. In the image on the right, taken just a few minutes later, as the Sun dips lower, less yellow is seen, as it has been refracted, leaving mainly orange and red. The red colour will be the last colour in the sky as the Sun sets.

Water and Sound

Sound waves travel faster and further underwater than they do in the air particles of the atmosphere. In water sound can travel at 1,500 metres per second, four times the speed measured in air. Sounds can come from earth movements such as earthquakes, tectonic plate movements, or movement of ice shelves, and from human activity such as submarines or surface ships. Animals such as dolphins and whales use sound in a system of echo-location used both for navigation and communication. Fin Whales and Blue Whales are well known for their 'whale song' which can be heard by animals over 5000km apart, and over 1,000m deep in the Atlantic Ocean. The whale's 'song' is very low, mainly below 50 Hz, so animal calls can be disturbed by SONAR (**SO**und **N**avigation **A**nd **R**anging) from navy and research ships.

Wave Energy

A cork bobbing about on the surface of the sea will rise and fall, but rarely moves forward. This is because the energy in the waves in the ocean move around the cork, rather than carrying it. The energy is in the wave which moves through the water. The water particles themselves do not get moved forward as the energy passes through. When you see a wave, you are seeing energy moving through water.

Waves are disturbances at the surface of the water created by the force of the wind. Wave size depends on the speed, duration (the length of time it is blowing) and fetch (the distance over which it blows) of the wind.

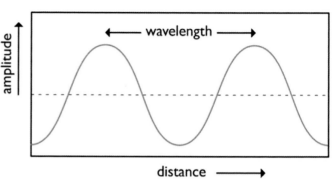

Wavelength and Amplitude

Waves can be described in terms of wavelength, and amplitude. Wavelength is the distance between the tops of each following wave, whilst amplitude is the maximum height of each individual wave.

The Rhythm of the Tides

The effects of tides cannot be seen in the middle of the ocean, but tides have an enormous influence on life in coastal areas. The simple explanation for the existence of the rise and fall of tides is the influence of the Sun, the Moon and the Earth's gravitational interactions. The Law of Gravity was described by Isaac Newton who showed that the pull of gravity depended on the masses of the bodies and their distance apart. He discovered that the force was 'inversely proportional to the square of the distance' – which explains that although the Sun is more massive than the Moon, it is much further away so its gravitational pull is less than half of that of the Moon.

Our tides are caused by a) the pull of gravity on the water which creates large bulges in the ocean. These bulges move to and fro every six hours, as the Earth spins on its axis, and b) a rotational force created by the spin of the Earth. The gravitational force of the moon creates an effect on the surface of the Earth nearest to it, which moves the water as a 'tide'. The rotational force, on the opposite side of the Earth, has a bigger effect than the gravitational force at that point, so the water in that area of the Earth moves in the opposite direction. Thus, the tide goes in and out depending on which part of the Earth is close to the moon during the combined movements of the rotation of the Earth and the moon's orbit.

The Sun has an added influence on the tides when the Sun moves into a position in line with the moon, strengthening the gravitational force, and creating very high tides (Springs) or very low tides (Neaps).

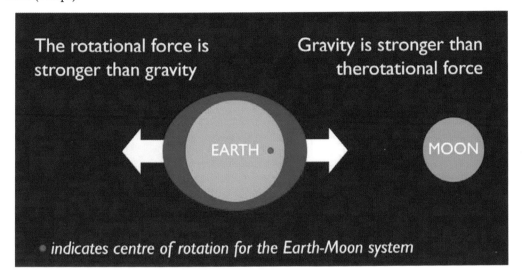

The rotational force is stronger than gravity

Gravity is stronger than therotational force

EARTH

MOON

• indicates centre of rotation for the Earth-Moon system

How tides are affected by the Sun and the Moon

There are occasions when flooding can occur, due to Spring tides being influenced by exceptionally high winds – such as the disastrous floods on the east coast of the UK and in Holland in 1953. London now has a Flood Barrier in the Thames to protect London in the event of these conditions conspiring again to create havoc. It is estimated that without the Thames Barrier, London would be at serious risk of flooding whenever there was a spring tide and storm force winds in the North Sea. Tides can also be affected by the shape of the adjacent land, or in narrow estuaries where tidal bores can be spectacular. The highest tidal range in the world occurs in the Bay of Fundy in Nova Scotia where the tidal range can reach up to 15 metres.

CHAPTER TWELVE

Atmosphere & Ocean - Currents and Climate

Atmosphere

There is a general agreement amongst scientists that the Earth was formed nearly 4.6 billion years ago beginning as just a collection of incredibly hot gases. Although scientific research is continuing and many arguments continue about the exact timing it is thought that by 4 billion years ago rocks had begun to form, and volcanoes were adding volatile materials into a primitive atmosphere.

The first atmosphere contained carbon dioxide, carbon monoxide, and nitrogen, and meteorites, containing ice, bombarded the early planet. The ice melted and formed water vapour. The vapour condensed to form liquid water about 3.8 billion years ago when the first ocean was formed.

Three hundred million years after the first ocean formed one-celled organisms started to release oxygen (O_2), and ozone (O_3) formed a protective layer around the Earth, keeping ultra-violet radiation from the Sun away from the Earth's surface.

The atmosphere is a layer of gases that surrounds the Earth and provides the conditions for life to survive. We are protected from the radiation of the Sun and from the showering of meteorites which burn up in our atmosphere on a daily basis. It contains our life-giving gas - oxygen - and provides us with the beauty of the colour of our sky. The atmosphere, however, is only part of our survival system as the Earth's atmosphere and ocean work together to create our special world.

Ocean water is constantly in motion, creating a dynamic and everchanging system. This continuous circulation of seawater creates currents which occur at both the surface and in the deep. The effects of the ocean currents influence the climate and living conditions for all life on Earth, both plants and animals, in both the sea and on land. This moving circulation of ocean water can create special climatic disruptions such as El Nino and La Nina, as well as being responsible for extreme weather phenomena such as hurricanes and typhoons.

Opposite page:: Stormy Seas

The ocean circulation and currents are caused by numerous effects all working at different times and at different intensities. All of the following factors are involved in our changing climate: Gravity, Earth Rotation, Solar energy heating both the Earth and its atmosphere, temperature of the water in different areas of the world, prevailing winds, salinity of the water, the Coriolis Effect and the shape of the bottom of the seabed – known as topography. These factors are explained in the following pages.

Thermal Radiation on Earth

As the Sun shines through our atmosphere the ocean absorbs most of the solar heat energy and creates a store of warm water. The heat is absorbed as the water surface is non-reflective. This warm water is transported around the planet by the ocean currents, and the world ocean acts like a giant heat transfer system.

More heat hits the Earth near the equator, as the Earth is not completely round, but is like a squashed ball with its top and bottom, at the poles, slightly pushed in. The equator is at the centre of the Earth in the bulge which sticks out around the middle, but the equator is not always the point which is the nearest to the Sun. That distinction is given to the 'subsolar point' which is the point at which the Sun is at 90° to the ground. The subsolar point is a moving point due to the Earth's movement in relation to the Sun, and it moves both north and south of the equator over the course of the year as the Earth orbits the Sun.

The radiation from the Sun penetrates the ocean only in the top 1 to 200 metres and a diver will soon start to feel the difference in temperature during the descent into the cooler water. The vast majority of the ocean never experiences sunlight and so remains extremely cold, between 4°C and 0°C, apart from around hydrothermal vents – but more of those later. Although some areas of the ocean at the extreme poles of the Earth may register as 0°C, the water carried there by the currents doesn't freeze due to its salt content.

Hadley Cells

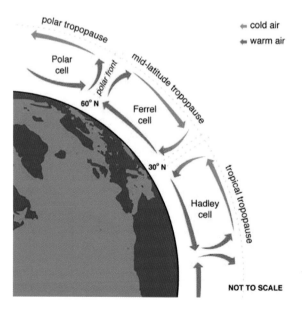

Solar heating of the Earth causes the gases in the atmosphere to move within three giant loops called atmospheric cells. Hadley cells are produced by warm air rising at the Equator. Ferrel cells are caused by the air cooling and then falling back to lower in the atmosphere in the subtropics as air starts to move north. Polar cells have air descending as it cools at the poles. The engine for all this movement of heat is the physical properties of gases – when air is hot it rises and when air is cooled it sinks. This movement of heat is known as a convection current.

High and Low Pressures

When warm air rises a low pressure is created beneath it, as the gases move apart and become less dense. When cold air sinks, a high pressure is created as the gases move toward each other. The change in density of the air particles is caused by the movement of the gases. When heated, gases gain more energy and move around more quickly, and they move away and upwards creating low pressure (fewer particles in the area). When air is sinking the density of the gases increases as the gas particles become more sluggish in the cold and get closer together (more particles in the area). When convection currents create high and low pressure, then wind is created by air particles being sucked in to fill the space in low pressure or moving out of the crowded area in high pressure. All of the movements of the air, and the atmospheric pressure at sea level relates to different weather patterns. A low pressure brings cloudy or overcast skies, lower temperatures and stronger winds whereas high pressure gives a period of stability with warm temperatures and clear skies. Weather systems, however, are notoriously difficult to predict.

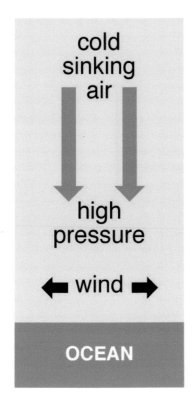
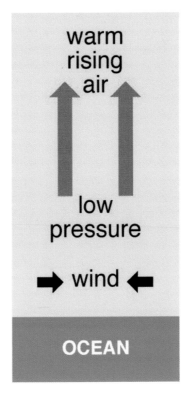

Convection Currents

The Earth's Rotation

The Earth spins beneath the airflow of the atmosphere. It spins continuously on its axis, completing a 'spin' of the Earth every 24 hours (one day).

This means that although you could be standing still on the equator, the Earth is still spinning, and you would be moving at a speed of over 1000 miles per hour (1500 km/h). If you were to walk from the equator to one of the poles however, you would move more slowly and by the time you get to the pole there is no speed in the circumference of the spin of the Earth at all. Growth rings on ancient corals suggest that there were more days in a year in the distant past. Fossil corals from 380 million years ago show 400 days in a year, so 21.8 hours per day, not the 24 hours we know today. And – the Earth is still slowing down – we are losing 2 seconds from our day every 100,000 years. It is thought that the slowing is caused by tidal cycles creating a 'drag' on the Earth's movement. So – oceans again are involved again and are responsible for this slowing.

The Earth's Rotation

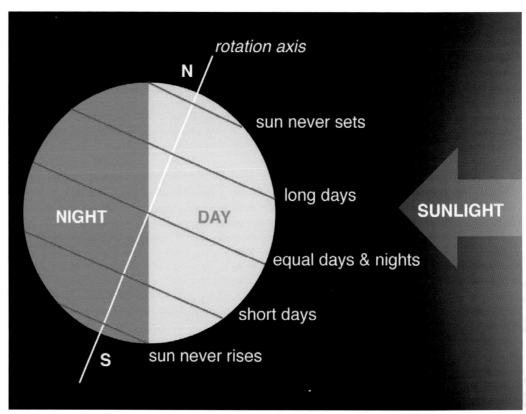

The Coriolis Effect

Gustav Coriolis (1792-1843) was a French engineer, mathematician and scientist. His name is synonymous with the Coriolis Effect, but he also coined the term 'work' as a product of 'force x distance' – which is a simple physics equation.

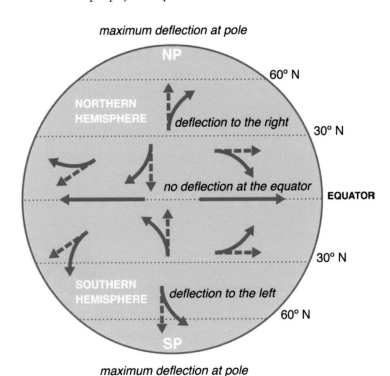

The Coriolis Effect

The Coriolis Effect, however, is not a force as there is no push or pull involved in it – only the apparent force exerted on the wind. The Coriolis Effect is an explanation of the way the air is deflected in the atmospheric cells in a North-South direction, as a consequence of the Earth spinning on its axis. However, as the Earth only completes one rotational spin a day the Coriolis Effect is extremely small and can only be seen in the atmosphere or ocean where it affects the largescale air and water movement.

If the Earth is separated into the top half – the Northern Hemisphere and the bottom half – the Southern Hemisphere – then Coriolis noted that winds and currents are deflected to the right in the northern hemisphere and deflected to the left in the Southern Hemisphere. So, at the North Pole the air gets deflected clockwise, and at the South Pole, it moves anti-clockwise.

101

Prevailing Winds and Jet Streams

The heat from the Sun creates 'pressure systems' of wind, and the spinning Earth creates the Coriolis Effect. Prevailing winds occur when both of these systems work together. Wind is always named after the direction if it is coming from. So, a North wind comes from the north, and a South wind comes from the south. When we start to look at water movement then we shall see that the opposite is true – and tidal streams and ocean currents are named for where they are going rather than where they have come from.

In the tropics the air movement in the Hadley Cell region is deflected to the west by the Coriolis Effect. Northeasterly trade winds occur in the Northern Hemisphere whilst Southeasterly trade winds occur in the Southern Hemisphere. In higher latitudes the Ferrel cells deflect to the east – producing the Westerlies. Seamen over the centuries have called these winds by different names, such as the Roaring Forties at latitude 40ºS, and the Horse Latitudes at 30º both North and South.

The origin of the name 'Horse Latitudes' is unknown but there are many versions of its origin. Here are some: a) horses on the way to the New World from Spain grew restless under still skies and panicked and had to be pushed overboard, b) it was the sailors who grew terrified by being forever stranded in still seas and jettisoned the cargo of horses in hopes of a lighter load and a faster journey (even today sailing ships try to avoid these areas, due to the lack of wind), or c) it is derived from the ritual 'beating a dead horse', where the seamen paraded a straw effigy of a horse around the deck representing the 'dead horse debt' – when the seamen had no income.

Prevailing Winds

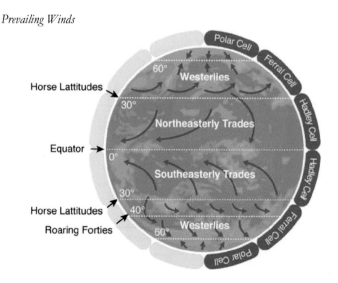

A jet stream is a bank of fast moving, high altitude air. They are usually westerly air streams and have been recorded at over 300mph. At the Earth's surface, air is slowed down by friction, but at higher latitudes the friction has no effect, so air travels faster. There are also pressure gradients in the atmosphere which are differences between areas of pressure, and the greater the difference the faster the wind speed. The polar jet streams are the best known and they occur in an area ranging in width of only 25 – 100 miles. Travel between the USA and the UK is quicker from west to east because the jet stream speeds up the journey.

Weather Forecasting

When all the air movements in the atmosphere are combined with the rotation of the Earth an incredibly complex air system around our planet is the result. Climatologists are constantly trying to predict the weather systems that all start with the Sun and the formation of convection currents. We have moved on a long way in our knowledge since we first discovered convection currents and the knowledge that 'heat rises'.

Ocean

Surface Water Movement

Solar heating causes water to expand. When water molecules are heated, they acquire a kinetic energy which allows the molecules to move around and expand. Just watch the top of a saucepan on a stove – before it is heated the water is still and level, but as it gets hotter, the water moves around, and seems to move 'up' the saucepan. This water expansion occurs in oceans all over the planet although in very small height increases.

Near the equator the water is about 8 cm higher than in middle latitudes. This causes a very slight slope and water tries to flow down the slope. Gravity gets involved and tends to 'pull' the water down the hill but because water has a surface tension which creates friction, the flow is slowed down again. Winds blowing on the surface of the ocean use friction to push the water and water piles up in the direction that the wind is blowing. A wind blowing for 10 hours across the ocean will cause the surface waters to flow at about 2% of the wind speed. In reality this means that in a small boat, or taking part in yacht racing, winds of 10 knots gives an extra push through the water of 0.2 knots which can be good news in a yacht race.

Cyclones and Anticyclones

Cyclones and anticyclones occur when air moves from one type of pressure area towards a different type of pressure area. The Coriolis Effect then modifies the movement and produces circular winds. When cold air sinks towards the ocean and forms an area of high atmospheric pressure (when the gas molecules are more densely packed together) then an anticyclone develops. However, when warm air rises it creates areas of low pressure (less densely packed with molecules), and cyclones, or 'depressions' occur. The Coriolis Effect pushes these winds into a circular motion which can create havoc as cyclones can move rapidly over the ocean and create changes in wind strength and direction.

Sea Breezes

Guess what – sea breezes work due to the presence of convection currents – being run by the fact that heat rises! Land heats up quicker than water – so during the morning the land heats up and by the coast, the air moves in from the sea creating a sea breeze in the afternoon. Although it takes longer to warm up than land, water actually retains the heat for longer – so later in the day, as the land starts to cool, the air above the water is warmer and that starts to rise, creating a space for the air from the land to move back over the sea. So, at night-time, travelling at sea close to the land – you experience a land breeze. Aren't convection currents wonderful?

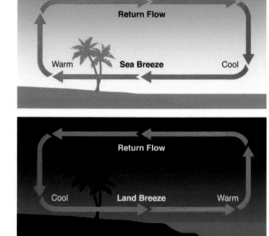

Far Right: Sea Breezes

Ocean Currents

There are two types of ocean currents – a) Surface Circulation and b) Deep Water Thermohaline Circulation. It is the wind on the surface of the ocean which affects the surface circulation- and these can flow for incredible distances, but wind has little effect on deep water. Although the wind causes the upper ocean to move, the water does not move in the same direction as the wind, as again the rotation of the Earth has an effect. The water circulation moves in a spiral, similar to the Coriolis Effect on the wind, but this time it is called the Ekman Spiral, after a Swedish Oceanographer V. W. Ekman. Discovered in 1902, the direction of the transport of the water is dependent on the hemisphere in which the movement is occurring. The Ekman spiral then predicts the movement of water in each layer of the upper ocean, using a combination of frictional drag from the wind at the surface, or the layer immediately above, and this model of water movement has to include the effects discovered by Coriolis. There can be a 90 per cent movement of the water away from the wind direction.

Ocean Gyres

Gyres are large-scale circulatory systems of currents which can be recognised by scientists and their progress followed. There are five ocean gyres, one in the Indian Ocean, two in the Pacific and two in the Atlantic Ocean. Each gyre consists of several named currents such as the Gulf Stream in the North Atlantic Gyre. As you would by now start to suspect, the rotation of the Earth creates opposite directions of currents in the northern and southern hemispheres, and the water can accumulate in the centre of a gyre – rather like water spinning down a plughole. However, a balance is created between the Coriolis effect and gravity which forms a geostrophic current. When all the forces are acting together, sailing on the surface water is more complicated than at first imagined. For instance, if travelling from the Caribbean Sea across the Atlantic to say – Madeira – then it is not quite as easy as travelling in a straight line. The currents would be trying to push a boat towards the south and the ship's navigator has to make constant alterations to the course to allow for this surface water movement as we cross the gyre. It can be a little bit like fighting your way uphill.

The ocean water becomes colder with depth, as the Sun's thermal heating effect dissipates the deeper in the water you go. Cold water also has a higher density than warm water, based on the same principles of density that gases undergo in the convection currents in the atmosphere. When warm and cold currents meet the denser water in the cold current moves beneath the water in the warm current. This creates a turbulence which produces an upward flow of water from the seabed. The water brings up nutrients from the lower levels of the ocean which feeds the plankton and fuels the food chain. The movement of the cold nutrient rich waters towards the surface of the ocean is known as up-welling.

There is a heat loss when warm water, such as the surface water in the Gulf Stream, moves across the North Atlantic and meets with colder water, such as the water travelling south from the Arctic, in the subpolar gyre. The density of the water increases and the water sinks. This is known as down-welling. This effect is also linked to salinity, with the water from the Arctic having a lower salinity than the water from the Gulf Stream, which has been evaporated in warmer seas and therefore has a higher salt content.

Down-welling also occurs in the middle of anticyclones where there is a spinning effect downwards. The cycling of nutrients through nutrient pumping systems of up-welling and down-welling is highly complicated and scientists are working to understand the directions of surface currents, using floats containing current meters.

Global Conveyor
The interaction of all the ocean gyres across the Ocean World gives the bigger picture. There is a slow moving, but very large-scale circulation of water called the Global Conveyor. It is estimated

that 50 million cubic metres of water enters the conveyor every second. It has been calculated that seawater takes about 2,000 years to complete a lap of this circuit.

The conveyor is fuelled by density and salinity differences which create a rise and fall of water as it cools and warms in different areas of the world. Scientists can track the direction of surface currents in many ways using fixed instrument moorings, and satellite information, although the

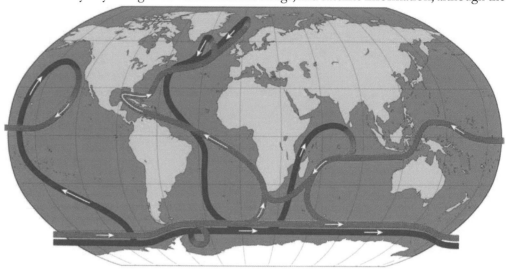

The Global Conveyor Circulation System

fixed instruments are quite costly, and often break free of their moorings in rough weather. There are some other rather unusual sources which have helped to produce data such as plastic ducks and Nike tennis shoes. Both of these incidents began with cargo ships losing their cargo in storms.

The 29,000 plastic ducks were 'released' into the ocean in 1992 when the ship they were travelling on was hit by a freak storm in the Pacific Ocean. The 'ducks' were small children's bath toys, and in fact were ducks, frogs, and turtles and have been acting as a floating science laboratory ever since. The ducks are expected to circumnavigate the world, and even end up frozen in Arctic ice. The 70,000 Nike trainers were knocked off a ship into the Pacific in 1990 and have been circulating the North Pacific gyre route ever since. Data collected from ducks and tennis shoes have been extremely useful in clarifying the movements of ocean currents.

Gulf Stream
The American inventor Benjamin Franklin (1706 - 90) completed an early study of ocean currents when he was asked by the British Postal Authorities why American postal ships could

cross the Atlantic faster than the British ships. Franklin investigated and found the answer in the system of currents in the North Atlantic which we now know as the Gulf Stream and the North Atlantic Drift.

Waters move eastwards from the Sargasso Sea and take warm waters across the Atlantic. If a ship gets caught up in these currents, then they can travel faster across the Atlantic. The Gulf Stream has a strong influence on the climate as it reaches the UK. Although the warm water does cool slightly as it moves north east across the Atlantic, it releases a great deal of heat and moisture into the atmosphere when it arrives in the UK, which makes the climate warmer and wetter than would be expected for the latitude.

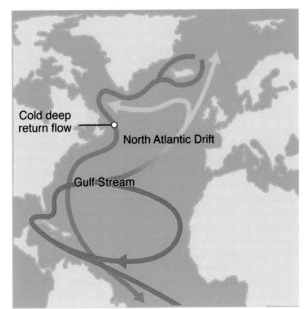

The Gulf Stream and North Atlantic Drift Currents

NASA are continuously supplying data for scientists from satellite information, and although it seemed that the Gulf stream slowed down in the 1990s, compared to the 1970s and 1980s, the fears of a mini ice age caused by global warming seem to be unfounded as the most recent research has found no long term trend, but just short term variability. Although the Gulf Stream might be expected to slow over the next 100 years, the cooling effect in the UK could well be offset by temperature rises due to other environmental changes.

Oceanographic research has also been carried out on the waters that pass between Greenland and Scotland where it has been discovered that over 8 million cubic metres of warm salty water passes through every second. This water is calculated to carry 300 million megawatts of power, 300 million kg of salt, and is responsible for the release to the atmosphere of heat which changes local climate.

Oceans Influence on the Climate
Hurricanes and Typhoons

Violent winds which start in a low pressure (depression) system over the warm waters of the tropics can develop into a circular pattern of movement, involving dense bands of cloud and rainfall. In the Atlantic they are known as hurricanes, whilst in the Pacific they are called typhoons. They occur mainly in late summer and can stretch to nearly 400 miles in diameter and be up to 10 miles high. At the centre is a calm region of low pressure known as the 'eye'. When a wind becomes stronger than 74 mph then it attains a hurricane status, with increasing force from category 1 to category 5 when winds can move at up to 135 mph. Hurricanes are pushed westwards by the prevailing trade winds, but run out of energy when they are no longer fed by the warmth of the ocean.

Climatic Disasters

El Nino and La Nina are large unpredictable climatic forces which act with reverse effects to one another. They are caused by abnormalities in the pattern of the temperature at the sea surface, together with changes in ocean currents and weather pressure systems. El Nino causes increased rain and floods in South America, or forest fires and drought in the Western Pacific, a reduction in the Peru Current, and disturbances in the hurricane season. It can last between 12 and 18 months, and although it is a cyclical event it does not follow a regular pattern, as it has intervals of between two and ten years. The effects of El Nino, and its reverse system La Nina, create devastation for humans when livelihoods are lost, food becomes scarce and lives are threatened.

Climate Change

There are some computer models of climate change which predict 'climatic' disasters and these get reported by the media, as well as films being made, like the apocalyptic Hollywood blockbuster, 'The Day After Tomorrow' – but scientists have a difficult task. Oceanography is a relatively new science, and there is not a century or so of data available, as we may have for other scientific disciplines. There are so many variables involved, that we still have difficulty in predicting the weather patterns for more than a few days in advance, let alone predicting global warming patterns for the next 100 years. Every day we are getting better at collecting data, but the Earth is highly unpredictable, due to the many natural forces at work.

CHAPTER THIRTEEN

Are there Really Mountains Under the Sea?

When the Earth Began

Our Blue Planet may seem calm and serene – but it hasn't always looked like this. The Earth was formed about 4.6 billion years ago, from a disc shaped cloud of dust and gases which orbited the sun. This cloud of gas condensed to form the Earth.

We know that solar energy heats the surface of our Earth, controlling the weather and hydrological systems of currents, yet there is another source of dynamic behaviour which affects our planet, the internal heat from within the Earth itself. Deep inside the Earth it is as hot as the surface of the Sun. Heat comes from decay of radioactive isotopes, gravitational energy and collisional energy. In the beginning, at the formation of the Earth, everything was molten, then iron silicates reduced to iron metal and sank to the core of the Earth. It is the iron content at the centre of our Earth that forms the magnetism which creates our Poles.

Seismologists (scientists who study earthquakes) have discovered the makeup of the inner Earth whilst taking measurements from earthquakes and have formed an image of the internal structure of our planet.

Seismic waves are waves of energy caused by earthquake movement. These waves come in two forms – P (primary) waves and S (secondary) waves. P waves are longitudinal waves which move like trucks in a train, being shunted and hitting the truck in front. S waves are transverse waves which move like a rope laying on the ground and being 'snaked' from side to side. These two energy waves travel through the rocks of the Earth by refraction and have different properties such as their velocities. Using seismographs, apparatus which records earthquakes, the scientists have calculated the speed of these waves as they travel through the Earth and by measuring the arrival times at different points on the surface, they can discover the type of material the wave has travelled through.

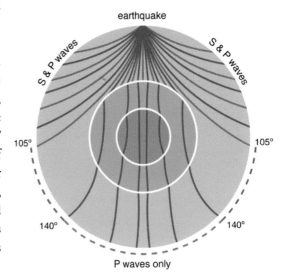

Due to these measurements we now have a image of the inner Earth – with its crust, an upper mantle, lower, mantle, outer core and inner core. The mantle is made of silicates and is solid, but it moves like a liquid due to the presence of water molecules. The outer core is liquid, and the inner core is solid. It is the spinning of the hot liquid in the outer core, containing iron, which creates the Earth's magnetic core. As this liquid moves it creates an electric current that creates the magnetic field around the Earth.

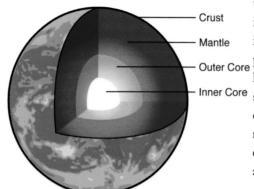

Crust
Mantle
Outer Core
Inner Core

Inside the Earth

The mantle, under the crust, is a solid which moves – and scientists believe it moves due to convection currents. As the heat from the core of the Earth rises, the mantle 'liquid' also rises, it cools as it gets further away from the heat at the centre of the Earth, and then the cooler 'liquid' sinks again – creating circular convection currents. The temperature at the core is over 5000°C, whilst under the crust it's only 1200°C. This moving layer is immediately beneath the crust of the Earth.

Far right; The Earth has a magnetic field

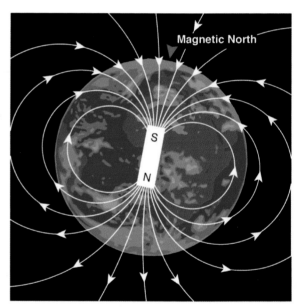

Magnetic North

S
N

The Earth's crust is the outside surface of our solid Earth, rather like the peel on an orange. The continental crust is the land, and the oceanic crust lies under the oceans. Sea water fills in the dips and holes in the oceanic crust and fills the ocean to 'sea level'. This level is controlled by the rotation of the Earth together with gravitation forces. 70% of the Earth's crust is oceanic crust, 65% of the crust is deep beneath the ocean, whilst 5% is shallow crust at the continental crust.

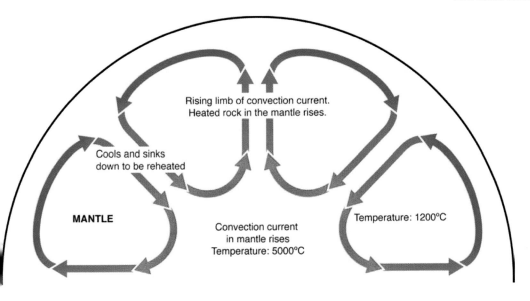

Convection currents in the mantle

Oceanic crust is made of young rocks, less than 200 million years old, whilst continental crust is older generally over 1500 million years old.

The oceanic crust is between 5 and 12 km deep, whilst continental crust can be up to 100 km thick beneath mountain ranges. The rocks found in the two types of crust are also different with ocean crust being formed from mainly basalt (a volcanic rock), silica and a large quantity of iron. Continental crust, however, is usually granite, silica with aluminium, and with a thin covering of sedimentary rock. All these differences have enabled geologists to piece together an understanding of what is going on under the oceans, and across the continents.

Oceanic crust - cross section

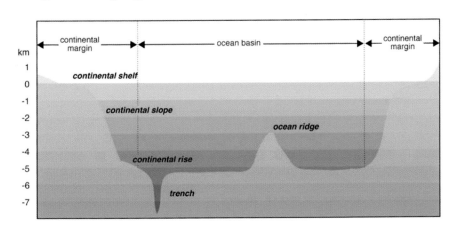

The Theory of Plate Tectonics

Oceanography is a young science, with James Rennell charting the currents for the first time in the early 1800s. HMS Challenger (1872-6) first explored 'below the waves', whilst it was post-World War II before oceans were really starting to be understood. Oceanography has only been studied for 60 years, although it was way back in 1915, that Alfred Wegener published his "Theory of Continental Drift". Wegener's theories were dismissed as fanciful at the time but the understanding of 'plate tectonics' was finally accepted during the 1960-70s when evidence started to be collected from different sources. The theory of plate tectonics states that "the Earth's outermost layer is fragmented into a dozen or more large and small plates that are moving relative to one another as they ride on top of hotter, more mobile material" – and that 'mobile material' is the mantle with its convection currents.

The main features of plate tectonics are these:

- Radioactivity, deep in the Earth's core, is the source of heat, which drives the convection currents in the mantle.

- The Earth's surface is covered by a series of crustal plates.

- The edges of the plates are not linked to the shape of the oceanic crust and continental crust but can be found both on land and under the sea.

- Convection currents in the mantle, beneath the plates, move the crustal plates in different directions.

- Plates can slide in opposite directions, pull apart or push together.

- The ocean floors are continually growing, spreading from 'constructive' margins, known as sea floor spreading.

- The area of the ocean floor is also decreasing at the boundaries of 'destructive' plates, as the oceanic crust is pulled back down into the mantle. or pushed underneath continental crust.

The Evidence for Plate Tectonics

There are three areas of scientific evidence which have led to our understanding of plate tectonics. Firstly, changes in Earth's magnetism, secondly, the distribution of volcanoes and earthquakes, and thirdly, the distribution of plant and animal fossils.

Earth's Magnetism

Scientists using research and survey ships, initially crossing the Atlantic, discovered 'sea floor spreading'. As ships crossed the Atlantic, they took measurements which produced evidence rather like a tape recording of the Earth's geomagnetic Field. This evidence showed that the sea floor had undergone reversals of the magnetic field – north moving to south, and south to north and that these reversals had occurred many times over millions of years. Researchers surveying the seabed revealed an area, now known as an oceanic ridge, with an identical magnetic pattern spreading out on either side.

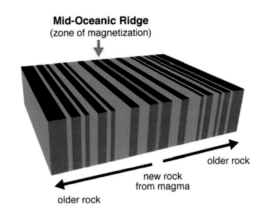

Magnetic reversals on the sea bed

Scientists started to realise that these mid-ocean ridges were gaps where new crust was being formed by hot magma from the mantle, rising due to convection currents. They concluded that these were the edges of two plates which were moving away from each other as the magma forced its way to the Earth's surface. Now known as 'constructive margins', the Mid-Atlantic Ridge was the first of these to be documented. Ocean ridges have now been found, all over the planet, at the margin between two plates that are moving apart. The magma forms the mid-ocean ridges or new volcanic islands – such as Surtsey Island, south of Iceland which lies on the Mid-Atlantic Ridge.

It was obvious that the Earth's crust could not just be growing in size all the time, or else the Earth would be getting bigger and there was certainly no evidence for that. So, the scientists started to look for evidence of subduction of the crust – where the crust moves back into the mantle, and they came upon another pattern to investigate.

Far Left: The Mid – Atlantic Ridge – a constructive plate margin

113

Distribution of Volcanoes and Earthquakes

As more evidence was collated, scientists started to see a pattern in the volcanoes and earthquakes which occurred around the Earth. This pattern formed the plate tectonic theories that could now account for 'destructive' plate boundaries where two plates move towards each other either on continental or oceanic crust. When two plates move together, then stress is caused in the rocks, which is released as earthquakes. Eventually one of the plates will be subducted and pulled down below the other plate into the mantle, where it melts due to heat and pressure. This occurs at areas of the crust called ocean trenches. The heat that melts the sinking crust comes from the interior mantle and from the friction caused as one plate rides over the other. As the magma, formed from

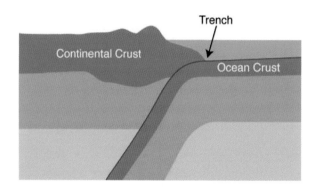

the subducting crustal material melts, it also becomes less dense. As this lighter magma rises above the subduction zone and into the rocks above, volcanoes are formed on the plate which is riding over the zone. Scientists were now able to use volcanoes and earthquakes to explain 'destructive' plate margins.

Distribution of plant and animal fossils

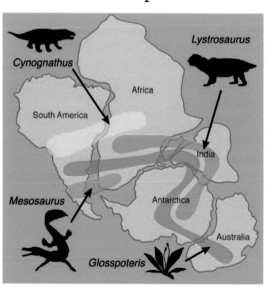

Studying the fossils on the different areas of continental crust has given scientists an understanding of the history of the Earth. Evidence has come from fossils of plants and animals found on two or more different continents showing that these continents were once joined together. There are fossil remains of a land reptile, Cynognathus, from the Triassic period of 200 million years ago which show the animal lived in both South America and Africa so it can be concluded that these continents were once joined together. Another reptile, Lystrosaurus, was found in Africa, India and the Antarctic, and the fern Glossopteris is found in all of the southern continents South America, Africa, India, Antarctica and Australia. This evidence shows us that the plates have moved over the surface of the Earth carrying the continents. Over 225 million years ago all the continents were joined as one large continent we call Pangea surrounded by one giant ocean called Panthalassa. Over millions of years the continents 'travelled' on the plates, fuelled by the engine of the hot mantle beneath them, until we have the map of the Earth we see today.

Movement of the Plates

The plates are still moving of course and will continue to do so due to the convection currents in the mantle. The Atlantic, which started to open up between the Eurasian, African, North and South American plates between 50 and 150 million years ago, is still widening at a rate of 2cm per year as the Mid-Atlantic Ridge (MAR) pushes up hot mantle from beneath the crust. Iceland, which sits across the MAR, was formed 24 million years ago yet still has many active volcanoes. In 2010, the Icelandic volcano Eyjafjallajokull became famous when it erupted, causing an ash cloud in the atmosphere which disrupted air traffic in Europe for many days.

The MAR is also responsible for the youngest island, Surtsey, which formed in 1963, and for an underwater volcano just 150 km south of Iceland which was discovered in 2008. This volcano already rises 100m above the MAR and measures over 50 km across.

The Red Sea is getting wider as it is formed at a constructive plate boundary between the African Plate and the Arabian plate. The plates in this area very clearly fit together, almost like a jigsaw puzzle.

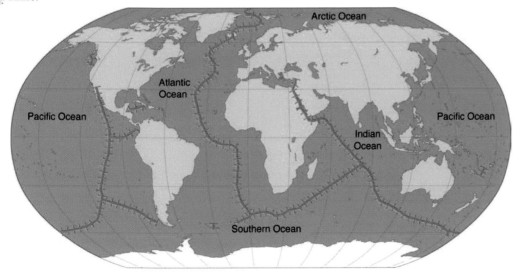

The main Constructive Plate Margins around the World

An area of Ethiopia, on continental crust called the East African Rift, was split open by forces of plate movement in 2006 when a gap appeared over 60 km wide in a matter of weeks. This area is a constructive plate boundary which is early in its development and is still overlain by continental crust.

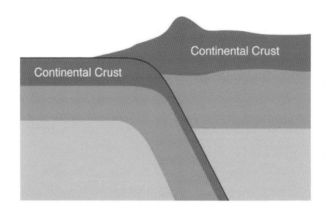

Continental Crust

Continental Crust

Right: When two continent collide mountains can be formed even when some subduction occurs as well

Plate movement caused the Haiti earthquake in 2010 as Haiti sits across a complex plate margin where the volcanic islands on the eastern margin of the Caribbean plate are converging with the South American Plate.

Mountains can be formed where plate movement forces continents to collide. The Himalayas have been formed from the converging Indian and the Asian plates.

Plates can slide alongside each other.

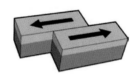

Plates also slide past each other and set off earthquakes. These are known as Transform Boundaries. Areas such as the San Andreas Fault, in the west of the USA, are famous for earthquakes caused as the stress builds up in the straining rock.

Recent scientific research however is showing that the seafloor in the Pacific off the western coast of the USA has been having thousands of small earthquake shocks, and it seems that the movement of the edge of the tectonic plates under the sea, close to the coast where the San Andreas fault is positioned, may be taking the strain out of the fault line – and the likelihood of earthquakes on the fault line itself may be fading.

The famous San Andreas Fault in the USA is caused by sliding plates

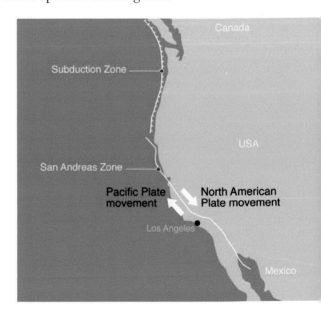

The mantle also has 'hot spots', and as plates ride over these areas, then island arcs are formed, such as the chain of Hawaiian islands.

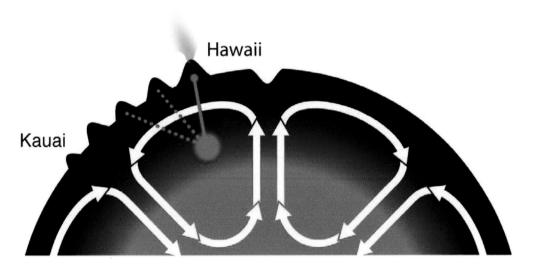

How the heat source from the mantle forms new islands such as the Hawaiian chain.

Seamounts, which are also volcanic in origin, are also found on oceanic crust near mid-ocean ridges or island arcs. They are mountains that have not risen above sea level. Madeira, in the eastern Atlantic, is a visible volcanic island that is surrounded by 'mountains under the sea' – the seamounts from an island arc.

The 'Ring of Fire' is situated around the eastern, northern and western edges of the Pacific Ocean. This area of destructive boundaries is where plates are converging and over 75% of the Earth's active and dormant volcanoes are located.

The epicentre of the earthquake recorded on 26th December 2004 was near the triple point junction of three tectonic plates – the Indian, the Australian and the African Plates. The earthquake was the second biggest ever recorded, and the shifting of the crust created a tsunami which was responsible for the deaths of over 250,000 people.

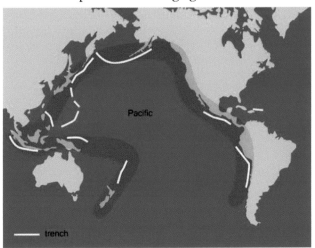

The Ring of Fire around the edge of the Pacific Ocean.

117

Tsunamis are waves which are usually set off by an underwater earthquake and are incredibly powerful as they hold onto the pulse of energy caused by the earthquake. Tsunamis can travel on surface water for very long distances and at very high speeds.

Tsunamis have a long wavelength but low amplitude, so they are often not noticed in the open ocean. When the tsunami reaches the shallow waters of a continental shelf, then the amplitude quickly increases as the seabed rises underneath, and this creates waves with heights up to 30m (100ft) which hit the shore creating terrifying destruction and disaster in their wake. The 2004 earthquake, which measured 9.1 on the Richter scale caused a tsunami in the Indian Ocean that killed people in 13 countries.

How a tsunami is formed

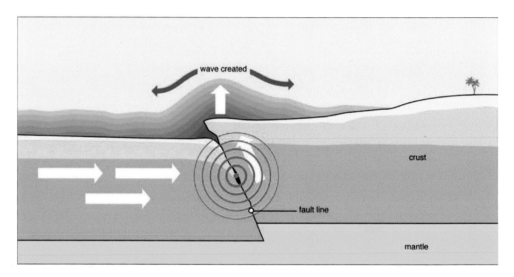

On Friday 11th March 2011 an earthquake occurred in Japan. Its epicentre was 80 miles from Sendai, occurring at 32 km beneath the ocean. The earthquake had a magnitude of 9.0 on the Richter scale, and was the largest earthquake in Japan's history. It was also in the top five of biggest earthquakes ever recorded. The earthquake caused a tsunami which destroyed vast areas of Japan and killed thousands of people. The tsunami was estimated to have been over 10 metres high when it reached the land. Thousands of people were reported missing, millions of buildings were destroyed. There was damage to infrastructure with roads and rail services damaged and one dam collapsed. Over 4 million people were without electricity and 1.5 million without water. Nuclear reactors became unsafe. Billions of yen were lost in the banking systems, and insurance losses were estimated at $34 billion. Japan declared that this was the biggest crisis for their country since World War II. The Earth was estimated to have shifted on its axis by 10 cm. It all started with the plate margins shifting and a human disaster was created.

Scientists still have lots to find out about the workings of the Earth. Do convection cells in the mantle really exist? Where and how do they originate? What is their structure? How do they change?

What we do know is that the Earth is a moving entity and humans have no control over the forces which control either the plate movements or the earthquakes and volcanoes which occur due to the activity of the hot mantle beneath the crust.

The Deepest Trench

Plates are subducting in areas such as the Mariana Islands, near Japan, where the deepest trench on Earth can be found at 6.8 miles (11km) below the surface of the Earth.

To understand the incredible depth of this ocean trench, perhaps it is wise to compare this depth with Everest, the highest land mountain on Earth, which stands at 5.49 miles (8 km) above sea level. There are also other comparisons, depending on how a mountain's height is measured. If measured from the crust, then the tallest mountain on Earth is Mauna Kea, in Hawaii. This mountain is an extinct volcano which rises from oceanic crust in the depths of the Pacific Ocean floor. From its base to its peak it is just over 10km in height, although only 4km of the mountain is showing above the ocean. Another measurement that could be used for measuring mountains is the distance from the centre of the Earth – in which case Mt. Chimborazo in Ecuador is the winner because it is 2,000 m further from the centre of the Earth than Everest due to its position on the bulge of the Earth at the equator. Whichever way the measurement of the height of a mountain is taken – it is still the ocean trench which wins the competition between mountains and trenches. Although over 4,000 mountaineers have reached the top of Everest, only a few men have dived to the bottom of the Mariana Trench. This was first accomplished by Jacques Piccard and Donald Walsh, who travelled to the deepest part of the oceans in a bathyscaphe called Trieste in 1960, and it was another fifty years before James Cameron in 2012 designed his own single person deep water capsule and stayed at the bottom for over 3 hours. In 2019 Victor Vescova became the first person to visit the deepest points in every ocean.

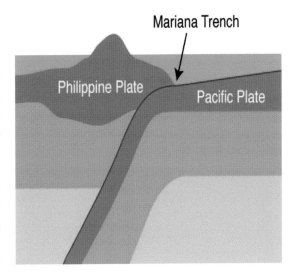

More men walked on the Moon in the 1960s and 1970s - 238,000 miles away (384,000 km) than have dived to the depths of our oceans at 6.8 miles (11km) down at that time.

Mid-Ocean Ridges and Hydrothermal Vents

Although we have only been to the bottom of the Mariana Trench twice, and although we have only observed about 1% of the seabed with our own eyes, scientific research of the oceans is uncovering the secrets of the oceans on a daily basis. The research vessels tow both manned and unmanned submersibles, they use high tech equipment and have radars to research the seabed. They have grabbers to take in samples and cameras to take images of new forms of life.

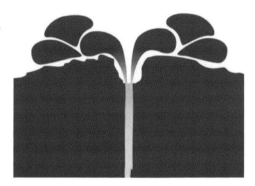

Scientists have discovered over 45,000 miles of mid-ocean ridges around the world. This makes these underwater mountains the longest chain of mountains on Earth. We have seen that new sea floor is continuously being added from the hot magma rising from the mantle and the new ocean ridge fractures and splits as the plates move apart.

Far Right: Pillow lavas forming on the sea bed at a constructive margin

Structures of rock known as pillow lavas are formed when hot magma emerges from between the plates and is smoothed by the quick cooling of the seawater. Pillow lavas are usually about 3 feet across and can be up to several metres long. At the centre of the spreading area on the ridge they can form small hills.

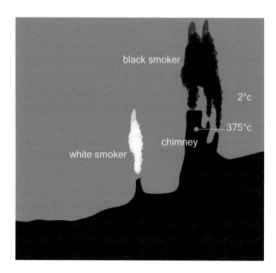

black smoker

2°c

375°c

chimney

white smoker

A 'smoker' on the sea bed

Seawater at 2°C filters through the fractures and becomes superheated by the 1200°C magma. The seawater then gets forced up through the fracture zone, carrying dissolved minerals from the magma and forming hydrothermal vents. The release of the dissolved minerals produces chimney like 'smokers' – sometimes black, or sometimes white, these smokers change according to the minerals being released from the magma. The mineral particles which are deposited form the stacks of the chimneys for the smokers.

120

Life at the Vents

Although hydrothermal vents and areas of hot erupting magma would not seem to be the ideal place to find life, scientists have found that areas around the marine hydrothermal vents are biologically very productive.

Chemosynthetic organisms have developed. These are creatures that make energy from chemicals (chemosynthesis) rather than from light (photosynthesis), and it is the chemosynthetic Archaea bacteria that is the producer at the bottom of the deep-sea food chain, which then supports other life. These bacteria can use hydrogen sulphide, a chemical which is highly toxic to other life forms on earth, to make their energy. Some of the life forms do not use oxygen (they are anaerobic), whilst others still require the photosynthetic organisms to supply them with oxygen for respiration.

The bacterial life forms at ocean ridges and hydrothermal vents have taken advantage of the warmth and chemicals released at these dark inhospitable places on Earth – and new species of life, often with a form of gigantism are commonly being discovered, such as giant tube worms, up to 8 feet long, and giant shrimps. These have been collected by researchers together with scale worms, snails, bivalves and crustaceans such as the 'eyeless' shrimp. Over 350 new species of life have been discovered at hydrothermal vents.

Some scientists are now suggesting that life on earth may have originated in these hot, chemically fuelled areas of the sea with the early bacteria being chemosynthetic, and that other forms of life evolved later once oxygen became available.

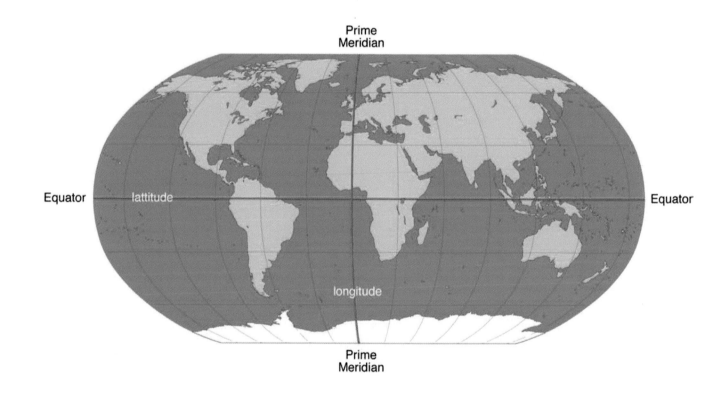

Prime Meridian

CHAPTER FOURTEEN
Poles Apart - Arctic and Antarctic

We live on our 'Blue Marble' planet, yet we have sunshine at the equator, and ice at both poles. What is it that causes these different conditions? Well, it is our old friend, the Sun, together with the Earth's position in relation to it. In our solar system the planets Mercury and Venus are too close to the Sun for humans to exist, whilst Mars, Jupiter, Saturn and Uranus are too far away. The Sun is exactly the right distance from Earth and supplies the right amount of light and warmth that we need. Different areas on Earth e.g. the poles and the equator change in the distances they are from the sun according to the tilt of the Earth towards or away from the Sun and the rotation of the Earth on its axis.

Latitude and Longitude

Latitude and longitude are the standard, geographic coordinates, measured in degrees, which we use to navigate around the world. They are angular measurements, calculated from the centre of the Earth.

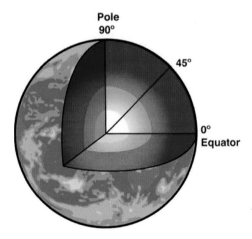

The equator, which divides our planet into the North and South hemispheres, is the starting point for measuring Latitude. Lines of Latitude are parallel to the Equator which is given a value of 0° at the equator leading up to 90° at the poles.

Degrees from the centre of the Earth

Longitude lines are the up and down imaginary lines that we use for coordinates. They are Time Lines, or Meridian Lines, which run perpendicular to Latitude and converge at the poles. There no obvious starting point for the 0° degree line, but historically, there was international agreement which gave the 0° to Greenwich in the United Kingdom. Thus, Greenwich is the Prime meridian and Longitude values are measured as degrees from the Greenwich meridian line, either east or west.

The Poles

Geographically our poles are at 90° North and 90° South and they have no longitudinal value. The geographic poles are known as true North or true South but just to confuse it all we also have a 'magnetic North pole' and a 'magnetic South pole' which are not in the same place as the true north pole, or the true south pole.

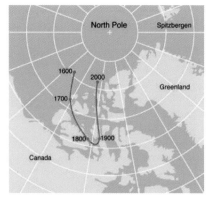

The Earth's magnetic field is constantly changing, mainly due to currents of metal inside the Earth's outer core, and partially due to charged particles flowing towards the earth from the Sun. These effects make the core of the Earth act like a giant magnet.

The compass points for the North and South Pole move continuously almost on a daily basis and since its discovery in 1831, the magnetic north pole has moved hundreds of miles before reaching its present position. Any navigation of the oceans requires knowledge of both geographic and true compass bearings and the differences between them at various parts of the world need to be calculated in order to stay on a correct course from one part of an ocean to another.

Estimate of Magnetic North

The compass points for the North and Pole position – over four centuries.

Weather at the Poles

The Earth is not a perfect sphere – it is wider than it is tall – giving it a slight bulge at the equator. The circumference of the earth at the equator is nearly 25 thousand miles (40,000 km) but when measured from pole to pole the circumference is 41 miles shorter. This shape is known as an ellipsoid (or, in the case of the Earth, a 'geoid', meaning earthlike). For us to understand the weather conditions at our poles, we need to look at the way in which the earth spins on its rotational axis. If a log rolled along the ground, it would move through an imaginary horizontal axis, but an ice skater, who is stretching upwards, will spin around an imaginary vertical axis. Our Earth doesn't quite do either horizontal or vertical – but instead it moves like a spinning top which is leaning over to one side. The imaginary axis of our Earth's rotation is at 23.5° from the vertical.

How the sun's rays hit the Earth.

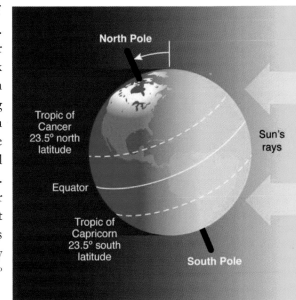

It is the 23° tilt which causes the Northern or Southern hemispheres to point towards or away from the sun at different times of the year. As the Earth orbits the Sun it creates the seasonal pattern of weather and climate and allows the poles to experience six months of daylight and six months of darkness every year.

The temperature arriving at the surface of the earth depends on the Sun's intensity. Although the total amount of sunlight is constant, it is the tilt of the Earth on its axis which changes the angles at which the sunlight hits the surface, which changes its intensity and subsequent warmth. The sun is more intense and warmer when it is at 90° to the ground at the 'subsolar point', and less intense and colder at the poles, due to the light being angled and spreading out over a larger area of ground the further North or South it travels.

The equator has the sun at its nearest point at an equinox, when the subsolar point is exactly on the equator and the sun has almost equal periods of day and night. The point at which the Sun is the furthest north, or south of the equator is a solstice, which is defined as a time when the difference is greatest between day and night time lengths. As the year progresses, the subsolar point moves northward towards the Tropic of Cancer, then, after the solstice it turns back south again, crosses through the equator to the Tropic of Capricorn, when the second solstice of the year occurs, and then it turns north back towards the equator.

The North Pole, however, is only tilted towards the Sun for 136 days out of the 365 day year, and for 91 days it is half in and half out of the light. This means that when the North Pole is tilted towards the sun – it becomes the 'Land of the Midnight Sun' as the sun never sets. The reverse, of course, happens in the winter period when the pole is tilted away from the sun, and for 136 days there is no sunlight at all.

The 'Arctic Circle' is an imaginary circle of latitude at 66°33'N which marks the southern limit of the summer and winter polar solstice, the point at which the sun does not rise in the winter, and the point at which the sun does not set in the summer. The Arctic Circle is about 1,600 miles south of the North Pole.

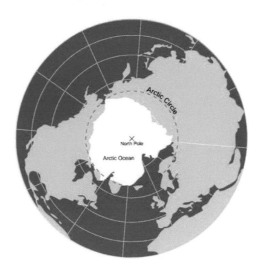

The Arctic Circle

125

The Antarctic works in a similar way – but of course at the reverse times of the year compared to the Arctic. There is only one day a year on the Antarctic Circle itself when the sun does not rise and another when the sun does not set. In between the Antarctic Circle and the South Pole there are up to six months of continuous darkness from March to September, and six months of daylight from September to March. The Antarctic circle is at a similar latitude to the Arctic Circle, but this time it is at 66°30'S – south, not north.

The Arctic Ocean

Roughly 8% of the size of the Pacific, the Arctic Ocean measures approximately 5½ million square miles, with a coastline of over 28,000 miles. The ocean includes the Barents Sea, Beaufort Sea, Chukchi Sea, E. Siberian Sea, Greenland Sea, and the North West Passage – but these are just lines on a chart. The North West passage stretches from Greenland in the Atlantic through to West Alaska in the Pacific with between 5 and 7 different routes through the archipelago.

Let us look at just one of these areas – the Beaufort Sea. The Beaufort Sea is north of Alaska and west of Canada's Arctic Islands. It covers 170,000 square miles and is named after an Irish hydrographer, Sir Francis Beaufort (1774 - 1857). Beaufort was an officer in the British Royal Navy, but he is most famous as the creator of the 'Beaufort Scale – which indicates wind force

The Beaufort Scale

Beaufort Wind Scale	Wind Speed (knots)	Wind Description	Wave Height (metres)	Sea Description
0	0	Calm	-	Calm (glassy)
1	2	Light Air	0.1	Calm (rippled)
2	5	Light Breeze	0.2	Smooth (wavelets)
3	9	Gentle Breeze	0.6	Slight
4	13	Moderate Breeze	1.0	Sight-Moderate
5	19	Fresh Breeze	2.0	Moderate
6	24	Strong Breeze	3.0	Rough
7	30	Near Gale	4.0	Rough-Very Rough
8	37	Gale	5.5	Very Rough-High
9	44	Severe Gale	7.0	High
10	52	Storm	9.0	Very High
11	60	Violent Storm	11.5	Very High
12	75	Hurricane	14+	Phenominal

aufort worked for 25 years as Head of Hydrography the British Admiralty and was an expert in using undings to find the depth of water. The information most of the charts and tide tables we use today were st collated by Beaufort and he also worked with the reenwich Observatory, making measurements of itude and longitude. He was really a very important an in the history of the charting of the seas and it is ting that he should have a sea named after him.

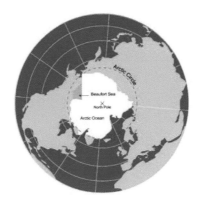

The Beaufort Sea

opography of the Arctic Ocean

he Arctic Ocean is the shallowest of all the oceans and when looking at the depths of these eans it is interesting to remember that most human recreational divers only go to a mere 30 etres.

he most important part of the dersea topography in the Arctic cean is the Lomonosov Ridge which vides the North Polar basin into two— e Eurasian Basin and the Amerasian sin. The Lomonosov is a fault block dge on a continental crust, which is her unusual. The ridge is 60,200 km de and rises to 3,700m from the ottom but which still leaves a safe depth water of nearly 1000 m at sea level for ips to cross it.

Ocean	Average Depth (metres)	Deepest Area	Deepest Depth (metres)
Arctic Ocean	1,038	Eurasian Basin	5,450
Atlantic Ocean	3,735	Puerto Rico Trench	7,725
Indian Ocean	3,883	Java Trench	8,648
Pacific Ocean	4,187	Mariana Trench	11,034

Average Depths of the Earth's Oceans

esources in the Arctic

2007 there was a descent to the North Pole seabed by a manned submersible by a Russian team no placed a Russian flag on the seabed at the exact position of the geographic North Pole. This uld be said to be the start of political discussions over who owns the seabed in the Arctic. It thought that there is an enormous amount of oil, natural gas and other resources to be acquired om the area in the future. The USA's Geological Survey has estimated that up to 25% of the orld's remaining oil and natural gas might be held within the Arctic region. At the moment there is no way that these resources could be extracted, but as the Arctic ice continues to melt, due to Global Warming, then the extent and thickness of the sea ice is diminishing, and it will soon become possible to search for oil and gas deposits. There are already signs that the North West Passage is opening during the summer and the Arctic could be ice-free in summer, by midway through the current century or earlier. This makes the Arctic a prize possession – but there could be many claimants to ownership of the Arctic.

In 1982 a 'Law of the Sea' was developed, which agreed navigational rights, territorial waters, exclusion zones, fishing rights, pollution rules, together with drilling, mining and conservation rights to 150 nations – and it gives a logical allocation of resources. However, the boundaries between the various seas, and the seabed on either side of the Lomonosov Ridge are contentious, with some countries trying to document the areas as extensions of their continental shelves and there could be many disputes to come over ownership of the Arctic seabed.

Ice

The Arctic, of course, is a world of ice. Ice is lighter than water – as there are more spaces between the molecules. When water is a liquid then it can flow, but its molecules are closer together than in ice, so it is denser than ice. The lower density of ice allows it to float on water. If there were two pots of equal size 10 parts of water could be measured into one, but only 9 parts of ice in the other – as ice is 9/10ths the density of water. When an iceberg floats around in an ocean, there will be only 1/10th visible above the surface and there will be 9/10ths of the iceberg submerged beneath the water – thus causing great danger to sailors and shipping.

Ice is also very strong – ice stops ordinary ships crossing the Arctic. Ships with special ice breaking features cannot force their way through thick areas of ice and although submarines can travel beneath the ice, they have to be very careful – using their sonar to navigate because if an accident occurred beneath the ice at the North Pole – then it would not be possible to attempt a rescue.

What would happen if ice did not float? Well, it would cause our world to change beyond recognition. Firstly, ice at the surface would sink, and the sun would not reach the bottom so the ice would gradually build up. Most seas, lakes and rivers would become ice. Life, as we know it would not exist in such an ice world.

Climate Change in the Arctic

Over time, small pockets of salty seawater get trapped in the ice, but the salt is squeezed out under the pressure of the weight of ice above it. Sea water in the Arctic has the lowest salinity of all the 5 major oceans. Due to low thermal temperatures there is little evaporation, and there is a high inflow of fresh water from melting ice. The Arctic also has a limited connection to the surrounding Oceans. Since the beginning of time, the Earth has undergone amazing changes, and over millions of years large continents have moved around the surface of the earth and split to make new continents. Ice ages have come and gone and today we are heading away from an ice world and towards warmer climates. Computer models of global climate are predicting considerable warming at high latitudes. Svalbard, on the Norwegian Spitzbergen archipelago, has been recording climate information for many years and their records show a 6°C increase in temperature in the last 100 years – our problem is that 4°C of that total has increased in the last 30 years alone.

Satellite imagery shows that the ice is breaking up and this brings a risk of extinction to our largest predatory mammal – the polar bear. These bears are totally dependent on sea ice for catching their prey. Starvation means that bears are not able to build up fat during the hunting season, and they are unable to survive the Arctic winter. Some scientists are worried that polar bears will be extinct by the mid-21st Century.

Global Warming

The warming of the earth at high latitudes is being blamed on global warming. The warming is also creating another problem – as when the ice melts in the Arctic the fresh water flows into the North Atlantic and dilutes the salty water. The reduction in salinity makes the water less dense and stops the water in the currents from sinking. Changes like these could stop the warming effect of the Gulf Stream and change the climate in northwest Europe.

The last period of warming occurred on the Earth over 10,000 years ago. The woolly mammoths became extinct as the temperatures rose and the vegetation changed.

It is estimated that the Earth 50 million years ago had an atmosphere where the CO_2 levels were much higher than today and similar to those predicted for our future world. The polar regions would have had flowering trees and animals such as primitive horses and large hippopotamus-like mammals living in swamps. The fossil record shows high summer temperatures and mild winters – as the present Arctic Sea ice melts – perhaps the Arctic will become tropical land again?

129

The Antarctic and the Southern Ocean

Whilst the North Pole is located on ice which floats over the Arctic Ocean, the South Pole is on land and its position is over 10,000 feet above sea level. The Antarctic is a continental land mass that has an area of about 14 million square miles and is covered with 98% ice over its mountainous terrain. The ice can be over 2 miles thick in places and it is estimated that the Antarctic contains 90% of the world's ice. The continent is entirely within the Antarctic Circle and is surrounded by the Southern Ocean which is formed at the southernmost areas of the Pacific, the Atlantic and the Indian Oceans. The Southern Ocean was recognised as a separate ocean by the International Hydrographic Organisation in 2000 and is known as the fourth largest ocean in the world. There are some organisations however, such as the National Geographic Society, that still do not classify the Southern Ocean as an ocean in its own right.

Antarctica is known as a 'cold' desert with its average temperature measuring minus 49° and the lowest temperature on Earth was recorded here at minus 89°C. Winds have been recorded at over 200 mph. It is the driest of all land on Earth due to the low temperatures, with only 20 cm of rain falling in a year, and unbelievably it hardly snows either. It has mountains, (the highest at about 3 miles high), and volcanoes which erupt from the frozen landscape, but it is a very bleak area of the with no permanent population. Scientists who stay at the South Pole station are cut off from the rest of the world during the Antarctic winter for over 7 months of the year.

Changes in Sea Level

Sea level has always been a changing factor in the history of our planet as Ice Ages have come and gone. There is, however, considerable risk to both human lives and livelihoods in the modern world if the sea level were to rise significantly, as the majority of industry and homes around the world are concentrated near sea level. If Antarctica's ice sheets were to melt, then it is estimated that the world's oceans could rise by up to 200 ft (60 metres) all over the world. There is far more risk from rising sea levels if the Antarctic ice starts to melt, than if the Arctic ice were to melt. In the Arctic the ice is floating on water and floating ice is already displacing its own volume in water so would not have such a disastrous effect on sea levels, but the Antarctic ice is mainly built up on land and if that ice melted then there would be a greater rise in sea level, although it is estimated that sea level rises would take place over a longer period of time. Another factor to consider is that as ice melts then the water will become warmer and thermal expansion in water will increase the volume of water. Once any initial melting starts then the process will speed up as the water continues to warm.

Predictions of time scales for any disastrous rise in sea levels are difficult to make and although there are many scientific views, few scientists are expecting any great changes in the Antarctic in the near future. It is different in the Arctic however, as changes in the ice cover in the Arctic are already causing concern.

Life in the Ice

Of course, the major difference between the Arctic and the Antarctic as far as life forms are concerned is that polar bears live in the Arctic and penguins live in the Antarctic so these two species of animal are never naturally found together.

There are very few animals which make their natural home in such cold regions, although some Antarctic fish have lived at between +2°C and -2°C for 5 million years. Antarctic cod have a special protein in their blood which acts as an antifreeze and are known as the best adapted animal on the planet for survival in cold conditions.

Ice fish found in Antarctica have no haemoglobin in their blood. Haemoglobin is present in the blood of most animals and it is responsible for transporting oxygen around the body. Ice Fish however, manage without haemoglobin as oxygen dissolves more quickly in cold water and the fish can obtain higher quantities of oxygen over their gills than normal fish. The lack of this red pigment in their blood, however, gives the fish a translucent, and strangely ghostly colour.

Both the Arctic and the Antarctic are feeding grounds for different species of whales – with a full-grown Blue Whale estimated to eat about 4 million krill per day every day for six months.

This amount of food energy is laid down as blubber, enabling the whale to go without food for several months.

Beluga Whales are found in Arctic waters. They are small whales, growing from 1.5m long at birth, to over 6 metres as mature animals. Although born a dark grey colour, by the age of 10 years they have turned completely white which helps with camouflage under the sea ice. Belugas have a thick blubber layer but have lost the dorsal fin associated with most other whale species. The loss of this fin enables them to swim more closely to the ice above it when hunting fish.

CHAPTER FIFTEEN
Future of the Oceans

Water has been a part of our Earth for at least 3.8 billion years - almost since the beginning of Earth history - 4.6 million years ago. The oceans of our blue planet distinguish us from other inhospitable planets in our Solar System and beyond – but the future of our oceans and life on our planet is now thought to be at risk.

Oceans have moved water in deep convection currents around the world, absorbed salts and sediments from the land, been responsible for changes in our climate and for millions of years they have remained stable. In recent years, however, more research has been conducted on oceans than ever before and worrying trends are being revealed. Scientists are starting to notice changes – BIG changes, and these changes are accelerating on an annual basis.

Some of the major problems that are being documented are rising levels of pollution, damage to coral reefs, decline in fish stocks, and changes in sea temperatures and water levels. These changes are not taking place over centuries but are being measured in decades or as annual changes.

In the 1960s the international community was just beginning to worry about the environmental problems on our earth. Oceans, and the preservation of marine environments were on the agenda at the 1972 Conference on the Human Environment in Stockholm, but little was achieved. By 1982 the UN Convention on the Law of the Sea, worked on a global approach to ocean problems and put forward a plan to protect ocean environments and control the rights to ocean resources. Over 142 countries have signed up to this 'constitution for the oceans', yet the future of the oceans is still at risk and there is a growing cause for concern.

Rising Levels of Pollution

Already two thirds of the world's population live within 50 miles of a coastline and by the year 2025 this is expected to increase to over three quarters of all humans on earth. By 2050 it has been estimated that the human population of the world could be as much as 9 billion people. With so many people living on our Earth it is inevitable that the present pollution of the seas will increase with serious consequences.

There have been some high-profile accidents in the oil industry over the past few decades which have obviously done immense harm to the marine environment, but the amount of damage from oil accidents is dwarfed by the pollution from other sources. It has been estimated that 30% of ocean pollution comes from the atmosphere, and 50% of the total ocean pollution comes from populations of humans on land discharging wastes into the sea. Humans are responsible for waste entering the seas by discharging sewage and industrial waste, sea dumping, run offs from agriculture, industrial mining, and urban areas, spillages, waste heat and radioactive discharges.

An immense quantity of atmospheric pollution, created by humans, is absorbed into the oceans. There is already visible air pollution in the form of smog hanging over cities around the world, and this polluted air moves across the oceans dispersing gas and particulates into the seas.

It is amazing that most of the pollution of the sea does not come from the main users of the oceans – those involved in maritime transport. There are well controlled laws relating to dumping at sea, and most users of the sea understand the importance of maintaining the marine environment.

Damage to Coral Reefs
Coral reefs are under threat from human pollution as well as natural phenomenon such as bio-erosion and effects of surging waves and storms. Human activity such as removal of mangrove swamps and deforestation creates sediment run-off close to the shore which adds to all the other forms of pollution that humans inflict on the sea. Added to the pollution, and natural erosion the reefs suffer damage from overfishing, souvenir hunting, the aquarium trade, coral mining, and anchor damage. Excess CO_2 is turning the oceans acidic and coral reefs are struggling to survive in the higher temperature waters.

Decline in Fish Stocks
Fish account for around one quarter of all animal protein in the human diet, and a large number of people throughout the world have fish as their only source of protein. Fishing is also a major source of employment but, it is predicted that there will soon be a major gap between demand and supply, if action to reverse the trend is not taken. There has been serious overfishing in some areas of the world of basic fish stocks, and fish numbers have been unable to recover. Fish farming is on the increase, but it is unlikely that this new industry will be able to make up the demand in the immediate future, especially in poorer countries. As fish stocks dwindle then prices rise, so low income families can no longer afford to eat fish. However, the future need not remain bleak as United Nations Food and Agriculture Organisation estimates that 'marine catches could rise by some 9 million metric tons if fishing pressure were reduced overall and juvenile fish were allowed to live longer before being caught'. The UN agency has

recorded success in Cyprus and the Philippines which show that substantial increases in catch can occur in about 18 months in tropical waters, when better management of the fish stocks is undertaken. So – if we know what has to be done - all that is left is to do it!

Changes in Sea Temperatures

Excess carbon dioxide in the atmosphere is the main cause of increasing global temperatures that affect the oceans. Burning of fossil fuels in cars, planes, power plants and industrial processes have all increased the levels of carbon dioxide, which then traps heat from the sun in the atmosphere. There are two other gases which contribute to global warming – methane and sulphur dioxide and these gases come from industrial processes as well as emissions from volcanoes and livestock.

The changing temperatures of the ocean affect our currents, such as the Gulf Stream which will affect climate change and, of course, global warming is having an effect on the ice in both the Arctic and Antarctic with predicted significant melting of ice in the near future.

Changes in Sea Levels

The history of the Earth has recorded many changes in sea levels, as well as recording Ice Ages, mass extinctions of animal life and continental drift with oceans changing in size and location around the world over millions of years. So, a changing earth is not something new. The difference now is that the changes that are predicted will affect all life on Earth.

Ocean Research

There are hundreds of scientific papers written each year from scientists all over the world working on areas such as

- fishery management;
- investigations into chemical contamination on turtle eggs;
- impacts of longline fishery on sea birds;
- impact on fish and invertebrates of oil spillage;
- the social and ethical implications of climate change;
- response of coral to projected temperature level changes;
- surveys of populations of sea life, infestation of predator species; consequences of predator-prey relationship changes;
- effects of increased temperature on reproductive performance of marine animals;
- toxicology studies on phytoplankton blooms

and many, many predictive reports looking at the possible effects of continued human pollution on the oceans in the future. These papers are helping us to understand the marine environment, and hopefully will enable us to protect our oceans for the future.

Human Impacts on the World's Oceans

Why is the Ocean so special? Our World Ocean covers over 70% of the surface of the Earth and contains 1.35 billion cubic kilometres of sea water. The World Ocean hides mountain ranges with more volcanoes than on land and it is deeper at the Mariana Trench, than our highest Mountain, Everest (measured from sea level) is high. The volume of the marine environment has 300 times more space for life than that provided by land and freshwater combined.

Life started in the oceans and there are 228,450 known species of animals living in the sea and likely to be between 2 and 10 million more still to be discovered. The smallest, mainly one-celled algae, float around in the water unseen by humans. These are the plankton – millions of different species, all photosynthesising. Plankton are considered by some scientists, as the most important organisms on Earth because they make between 70% of all the oxygen that is on the Planet and it is oxygen of course, that supports all life on Earth. It is estimated that these tiny algae grow to total as much as 200 million tons every year – which is ten times the mass of the whole world's human population.

The oceans are also a vast barely touched resource and humans are only just starting to discover what the oceans contain and how useful they can be to us all.

The oceans are still producing new forms of life. Recent discoveries by scientists working with sponges, have given hopes for new cancer cures to be developed from the sponges.

Why the Ocean is Important to Humans

Apart from the plankton providing us with so much of Earth's available oxygen, the oceans also provide an amazing amount of protein food energy. Often fish or other marine life is the only protein that some people can source. Then, there is the world economy, of course, from jobs in fishing to ferries, or ocean-going transport with its important trade links around the world. Oceans dominate the world's climate by driving the three major global cycles – the water cycle, the carbon cycle and the energy cycle.

Water Cycle - Water is taken from the oceans by evaporation, forms clouds and travels around in the atmosphere. When temperatures change, then the clouds release the water as rain which drops to the earth. Without this water supply on land, there would be no life on earth. The water finds its way back to the oceans via rivers and the cycle starts again.

Carbon Cycle - When fossil fuels are burnt by humans, or volcanoes erupt, then the carbon dioxide goes into the atmosphere. The oceans absorb more than 50% of the carbon put into the atmosphere in this way. The oceans absorb the carbon, which is then used as calcium carbonate by marine creatures for making their skeletons or shells. When these creatures die, their carbon skeletons drop into sediment and eventually it gets made into sedimentary rock, which is often uplifted over millions of years to form chalk cliffs. Rain can wash the carbon from the cliffs back into the oceans. However, the carbon cycle is clogging up and there are serious consequences building up for the future.

Energy Cycle – All our warmth comes from the Sun, and the oceans keep the temperatures on Earth stable. Ocean currents carry water from the tropics to the poles, taking warm surface water deep into the oceans, and returning the cold water back to the surface. These important currents are responsible for the climate that exists on our continents. The currents also recycle the nutrients from deep under the waves back to the surface to supply food energy for the mass of living creatures living in the top 200 metres of the oceans.

Protecting our ocean environment is therefore unbelievably important to all life on earth – yet the oceans, despite their size, are seriously affected by the human impacts of pollution and the excess use of fossil fuels.

Effects of Pollution on Marine Life

The enormous gyres of plastic wastes now in our major oceans, are only there due to human activity. The plastic litter is now everywhere – even in the Arctic. Plastic is not bio-degradable, and it takes years for it to break down into the micro-debris which is also floating unseen in the oceans. These small pieces of plastic debris are being mistaken by birds for food, and it is being fed to chicks, killing them from lack of nourishment. Marine mammals, such as seals, dolphins and whales, together with sea birds are becoming entangled in plastic nets and other rubbish killing thousands of marine animals every year. Our rubbish is killing ocean life at an alarming speed. Raw sewage is still emptied into the oceans from human populations all around the world, putting more toxins that can cause disease into our oceans. More marine animals die, and the oceans have become toxic for fish with the poisons building up in the food chains – which will eventually be food for humans too. There are problems with overfishing and with fishing methods that are killing marine animals. There is horrific sound pollution from seismic air-gun testing, used by engineers to find oil and gas which are killing vast numbers of animals such as dolphins and whales. Aquaculture can be a problem if it is not carefully managed. Fish farms can spread disease into wild populations or release drugs such as antibiotics into the oceans in large quantities if they are not managed carefully. Industry isn't always clean – there are still factories in less industrialized countries where they are using mercury in their production of chlorine and releasing this deadly poison into the oceans and into the food chains. Oil pollution from accidents or spillages continue to endanger life, and then, of course, there is excess carbon dioxide being released into the atmosphere by the use of fossil fuels, which is being absorbed by the oceans.

Effects of Pollution of Human Lives

It seems that humans have now polluted the Earth to such a point, and we are now affecting our climate to such a level - that life on Earth is under threat.

If human activity was not part of our Earth, then the Earth would cope with the earthquakes, volcanoes, storms, droughts and changes in climate that are a part of this natural world. The Planet has always changed over time – but that time scale of changes was incredibly large with changes occurring over millions of years and all those natural changes were part of this living planet. Human pollution has speeded up, by thousands of years, the natural climate changes which would have occurred on Earth if humans had not been part of the scene. Human activity has changed the speed of change – and these changes are happening so quickly that there is a risk to all life on Earth unless we take action soon.

Climate Change Now

The effects of human activity, mainly the use of fossil fuels which produce the poisonous gas CO_2, has changed the speed of change on our Planet. Instead of taking thousands of years for climate to change – it has taken just a few hundred years of industrialised human impact to threaten the life we have on Earth. It has been estimated that major changes will occur in our climate by 2030, and that by 2100 temperatures across the whole of our Planet (not just the tiny weather patterns we see as we experience summer or winter) will rise by 3.6 degrees C to 5 degrees C. This may seem a small amount of change, but over the whole of the surface of the Earth it is a vast increase, and it is an increase that without humans, the Earth would have taken thousands of years to achieve, allowing time for creatures to adapt to the changes and survive. The temperature rise, expected by the mid to the end of this 21st Century, will cause droughts, and floods, and food shortages, whilst sea levels will rise causing island countries to disappear and displace populations.

Why should we think climate change even exists when we can't see the problems. When the sun is shining and we look out across a beautiful Earth, full of natural beauty, why should we be listening to all these worries from the doom and gloom merchants. Climate change – nah – let's all stick our heads in the sand and pretend it isn't happening.

Unfortunately, though, it is happening. The facts are now proven – there is no time for discussion anymore. The climate is changing, and unless we start to do something about it soon, it really is going to be too late to save life on earth from unbelievable and disastrous changes.

What are the facts in simple terms?

Fact 1 – too much carbon dioxide in our atmosphere. CO_2, caused by human use of fossil fuels (burning of coal, gas and oil) is warming the Earth's surface and is affecting the climate and creating global warming. CO_2 in our atmosphere traps the warmth of the sun, and the Earth is warming up at the surface.

How does Fact 1 affect life on Earth? The physical effects of excess CO_2 will be noticeable to humans in less than 50 years. It is estimated that even by 2030 we will be experiencing storms, and floods which will destroy countries and displace human populations. Millions of people will be displaced, lives will be lost. Melting of ice from the Arctic will affect ocean currents, such as the Gulf Stream (which gives the UK its mild weather), and weather patterns across the Earth will change leading to droughts and food shortages.

Fact 2 – the oceans are becoming acidic. The amount of atmospheric carbon dioxide, from human emissions such as burning fossil fuels, means the oceans are absorbing more and more carbon dioxide. The oceans are absorbing up to a million tons of carbon dioxide every hour. The increased carbon dioxide is turning into carbonic acid and, known as ocean acidification, this is now killing life in the oceans.

How does Fact 2 affect life on Earth? Ocean Acidification is affecting the survival of those incredibly tiny, one-celled creatures called plankton - those creatures that are so small you cannot even see them in the water. There are millions of them floating around in the top 200 metres of the oceans. The plankton in our oceans provide us with 70% of the oxygen in Earth's atmosphere and if there were lower oxygen levels, then all life on Earth would be at risk.

Small but essential creatures such as pteropods and krill play a crucial role in ocean food chains, but they are dying due to acid attacking their shell structure and it is all happening so quickly that these creatures have no time to adapt to the new acidic conditions. Humans will see food shortages, as seafood industries are also being seriously affected by ocean acidification.

Global warming and Ocean acidification – these are 'twin evils' for which the facts are undeniable. The Earth is a very big place, and as individuals we can't see the damage that is occurring from the excess CO_2 gas, but it exists. It is real. Climate change is a real threat for all of our futures, and the futures of our grandchildren's children.

What will happen to Human Populations?

Climate change - What will be the real and visible effect on humans? If you have ever seen pictures of mass starvation in Africa after the droughts, then you will understand the devastation such droughts cause for human populations. Human populations all over the world will be affected by flooding, droughts and changes in weather patterns at a local level. Sea level rises will create displacement of human populations from island states, and some of those island countries will disappear completely.

Reduced oxygen levels - Without the plankton, oxygen levels will reduce in our atmosphere and all life forms, including humans, will be threatened.

Food shortages – The oceans at present provide immense quantities of human food resources, but food from the ocean will become scarce as plankton and krill won't be fuelling the food chains and creatures higher up the chain will die.

Humans need to start believing that they can do something about climate change. Excess carbon dioxide emissions and ocean acidification are damaging our atmosphere and our oceans now. These are not just changes which will occur suddenly in 2030 – it is already happening. Humans, especially those living in developed countries, need to stop denying that carbon dioxide is poisoning our Earth and acidifying our oceans – it really is happening already. Humans can start to reverse these effects if action is taken now to reduce fossil fuels.

Scientific research has shown that effects on coral of ocean acidification can be reversed. If the use of fossil fuels can be reduced, then carbon dioxide will decrease in the atmosphere and the oceans. Reduced carbon dioxide emissions will mean that the oceans can start to recover.

The oceans need to be healthy and produce food and oxygen or life on Earth will change forever, for every species on Earth, including humans.

Reducing fossil fuel use and consequent carbon dioxide emissions is highly achievable as the technology is already available to become a fossil fuel free world. Economic priorities need to be reconsidered, available clean energy technology needs to be used more widely, and continued research and development will make these systems even more efficient

This needs to be done now, if life on Earth is to survive. Humans need to stop prevaricating, learn about our Earth and the problems of fossil fuels and then educate people across the world in how to look after our Planet.

Human Survival

Climate change, at the moment, is like a stone on the edge of the hill. If control is lost, the effect will be like rolling a stone down a hill – once started it will gain momentum. Humans are very clever – they have invented their own 'human' world of economies and wealth, politics and sometimes even peace – but now it is time to face up to a bigger challenge – human survival.

These words may sound dramatic – but they are needed if humans are to understand the major problems which are facing them. At the beginning of 2014, politicians around the world were in denial. The new Government in Australia had just cut the carbon tax, the USA uses shale gas instead of looking for clean energy, whilst poor non-industrialized countries are being sold yet more coal from the US and Australia. Just days after the 2013 publication of the most important scientific document about climate change was published by the Intergovernmental Panel on Climate Change Report (IPCC) – a prominent UK Government spokesmen was speaking of using the extraction of shale gas, by the process of fracking, as a solution to energy needs in the UK. Yet again, a politician has missed the point – shale gas is a fossil fuel and as it has been pointed out yet again, by the latest IPCC report, it is the human use of fossil fuels that is mainly responsible for the increase in carbon dioxide levels leading to the serious changes in our atmosphere and oceans. Governments should be leading the way to finding alternatives to the use of all fossil fuels – not just turning to 'different' fossil fuels such as shale gas.

The IPCC (2013) recommends that carbon dioxide emissions worldwide be reduced by 50% by 2050. However, ocean scientists are already finding that the acidification is more serious than first thought and a 60-70% target of carbon dioxide emissions could be more appropriate.

Targets are needed for communities around the whole of the world:

1. Governments of the world need to work together to put human survival at the top of the agenda and be innovative in developing clean energy policies.
2. People need to learn more about what is happening, and then educate others to understand why excess carbon dioxide emissions are a threat to all life on Earth.
3. Individuals need to influence thinking, and work together as local communities, to ensure that the politicians are working towards a world free of fossil fuels.
4. Fossil fuels need to stay in the ground everywhere around the world.
5. Sales of coal must be curtailed to the poorer countries within a specified target.
6. Governments of the world need to announce that low or even zero emissions of fossil fuels, in all industrialized countries, needs to be achieved in 10 years. Industrialized countries need to help the non-industrialized countries where a total of 2.5 billion people lack access to modern energy, and include those people into eventual zero emissions of fossil fuel schemes and improve their quality of life without further damage to the Earth.

The situation in the world now is a little like the situation in 1961, when President Kennedy set the target that the USA would put a man on the moon. When it was announced, there was hardly any technology available to achieve that target. Yet, it took only 8 years for the scientists to provide the technology to achieve that incredible feat, and the technology they produced in that time span was astonishing. If a challenge was set now, to stop using fossil fuels within 10 years, then scientists around the world would produce all the technology needed in the time span. Most of it is already in existence.

How could communities work together?

It needs local communities to take a lead over what is happening in their areas and not to accept the shrug off attitude of others that there is 'nothing we can do' - because it is possible to get things done locally and influence decisions. Already there are local communities in the UK working together to provide local clean energy sources from wind, solar, geothermal, biomass and other clean systems which are enabling those communities to take a lead. Governments need to be encouraged to help local communities to acquire the technology needed. Within the industrialized countries communities firstly need to look after themselves and develop schemes which are appropriate for their area. Whether individuals live in a village, town or city it is possible to start to work together to become self-sufficient in energy through clean energy systems. Once we have good working systems in local communities then it should be possible to look further afield and each community in an industrialized country could adopt a community in a non-industrialized country in order to help them to become self-sufficient in energy too. Individuals would then be understanding and working towards a 'planet' solution. It is possible to do this but what is needed is for humans to stop hiding their head in the sand and actually get the will to do what is needed. By starting with local communities, it is possible to move forward and help others around our world. Humans need to become citizens of Earth – global citizens – helping each other to achieve an Earth fit for our habitation.

Can the Earth Recover?

By drastically reducing the world's carbon dioxide emissions as soon as possible, then the ocean will once again be able to absorb the excess carbon dioxide from the atmosphere. This will reduce the warming effect and consequent climate change that will happen to our Earth if nothing is done. The oceans can recover from the acidification they are suffering now, and healthy oceans once again will be working in a natural way on our Earth.

The mess of pollution – sewage, plastics, sound and all the other horrific elements from the waste produced by humans must be legislated for, cleared up and again the oceans returned to a natural clean state.

What is the alternative to these ideas - can humans carry on as they do now, polluting and poisoning our Planet? If that happens, then life on our Planet will be destroyed. The Earth is home to a wide variety of species, including humans, and the damage being caused to our Planet could render all life on Earth homeless. Humans could not survive in the extreme conditions of climate change, and ocean acidity. In less than a hundred years our Earth could be unbalanced by excess poison gas, and our oceans could be dying. The Earth could be totally devastated by reckless human activity, and 'life' would become 'survival' beyond our imagination.
Second edition – February 2014
READ ON for comments in 2021 in the THIRD Edition

Third Edition – March 2021

Updating this chapter today, I realise that the words I'd written five years ago are all still relevant.

Although in 2021 more people understand the problems with pollution of the Earth by plastic, and also understand the need to stop using fossil fuels because of the dangers of excess CO_2, we are a long way away from seeing the required changes happening fast enough if life is to survive on our planet.

There are good and responsible people who are bringing the Earth's problems to the forefront of our minds - Greta Thunberg - representing those young people across the world who will inherit our mess. (If you haven't done so already – then look her up on YouTube and listen to her speeches.) Greenpeace, Friends of the Earth and the United Nations are all shouting out what needs to be done too – yet not enough of us are listening and acting on what we hear?

There are people in high public places in politics around the world who are denying the very existence of climate problems. The world we know is changing, yet do we have the time left to save our planet? The Earth has been described as working as a giant feedback loop – but it won't be long before humans will have done so much damage that we'll have reached a tipping point when the feedback loop will stop feeding back and we will hurtle into a catastrophe that is unstoppable.

We must take our future seriously – listen to the protesters on the streets of the world, they have got it right. We need to act NOW or the Earth as we know it will be destroyed – with all life coming to an unimaginable end.

Gloria Barnett
March 2021

Acknowledgements

The author wishes to thank the following for their contributions:-

NASA Images © public domain
Page 11 - Earthrise: NASA Photo Library http://visibleearth.nasa.gov
Page 12 - The Blue Marble: NASA Goddard Space Flight Centre
Page 46 - Giant Squid
Page 50 – Great Barrier Reef

NOAA © public domain
Index p5 - Underwater Mountains- McMurty - NOAA
Page 21 - Hydrothermal Vent
Page 28 - Pufferfish
Page 28 - Cowrie
Page 33 - Diatoms in Antarctica (Prof Gordon T. Taylor)
Page 40 - Sea Cucumber (David Burdick)
Page 40 - Flatworm (Dr.J McVey)
Page 42 - Dolphin
Page 46 - Giant Isopod
Page 46 - Blobfish

US Dept of Agriculture © public domain
Page 27 - Cow

Other © public domain – copyright expired
Page 24 - Finches - John Gould – 'Voyage of the Beagle' 1845 .
Page 44 - Angler Fish - August Brauer 1906
Page 44 - Vampire Fish - Carl Chun, 1911.
Page 46 - Fangtooth - "Oceanic Ichthyology" by G. Brown Goode and Tarleton H. Bean, published 1896

The following seven images have been generously shared through **Creative Commons** (www.http://creativecommons.org)
Index p.4 - Sea Slug Alexander Jenner
Page 27 - Zooplankton - Øystein Paulsen
Page 28 - Jellyfish – Hans Hillewaert

Page 28 - Crustacean - Hans Hillewaert
Page 35 - Red Sea Coral - Haplochromis
Page 49 - Copepod - Uwe Kils
Page 61 - Flatworm - Richard Ling
Page 78 - Sea Snake - Jens Petersen
Page 81 - Seal - L Heafner
Page 84 - Marine Iguana - Kjersti Holmang

Diagrams and Charts
Tiki Graves - All diagrams and illustrations (tikigraves@gmail.com)

Photographs
The author would also like to thank all the highly talented divers and other professionals who generously contributed their photographs.

Chris Barnett – page 39 bottom, 56 bottom, 67 top middle, 69 top middle
Gloria Barnett – page 17, 18, 27a top, 36, 37, 68 bottom, 93 x2.
Charlotte Best – page 27a bottom, 28 a,b,c, 39 top, 47
James Burford – page 27d, 69 bottom middle, 74
Joshua Rainey Photography - page 96 courtesy istockphoto.com
Lee Rogers - page 132 courtesy istockphoto.com
Matthew Burford – page 86
Emma Button – page 20
Anna Georgetti – page 62 bottom, 69 top L, 77
Ian Gibbs – page 80
Tiki Graves – page 30, 51,53,56 top L & middle, 58, 60 bottom, 63, 66 bottom, 67 top L, top R, middle R, 69 top R, bottom R, 72, 73.
Lindsay Herrington – index (cuttlefish), page 9, 10, 55, 60 top, 61 bottom, 64 bottom, 67 middle L.
Sian Herrington – page 25, 28 g,i,k,m,54 left x 2, 64 top, 66 top, 76 bottom.
Steve Jones – page38
Ryby Stonehouse – page 8, 14, 23, 27c bottom, 28 j,l, 35 top, 40 top right, middle, 41, 54 left, 56 top right, 62 top, 67 bottom, 69 bottom L, 70 L & R, 71
Dray van Beecke – page 59, 62 middle, 68 top, 76 top, 82

Index

A

B

C

D

E

F

P

R

S

Working to Inform Children and Adults
Speaker and Author

Gloria Barnett is dedicated to helping inform young and old
about Planet Earth and its Ocean

Speaker:

Gloria is a science educator with a special interest and a lifetime's experience in exploring the oceans. She presents oceanography talks, including original film, to audiences all around the world, speaking to young and old about our planet and its' amazing sea life.

Author:

Gloria's non-fiction book – 'The Amazing World Beneath the Waves' is a fully illustrated and accessible guide to the oceans. Suitable for ages 10-110!

Gloria's series of children's fiction books

The Lucy Morgan Adventure Series: for ages 8-12

Book 1 - 'Eye of the Turtle' - was published in May 2020
When Lucy leaves London for a new life in the Caribbean she becomes intrigued by life under the waves and promises to help protect the creatures which live in the ocean.

Book 2 - 'The Secrets of the Shallows' was published in August 2020,
Together with her new friends Sol and Jack, Lucy continues to get into dangerous situations whilst looking after the ocean creatures she loves.

Book 3 - 'The Hidden Cave' was published in November 2020.
Lucy, Sol and Jack get entangled in yet another challenging adventure, as they battle to protect marine animals.

All these books not only deal with animals, nature and environment but also help children understand they can 'make a difference'!

All books are available from the website -
www.barnettauthor.co.uk
or from
www.footprinttothefuture.co.uk

Gloria's early-reader's children's fiction books -

The Fishy Tales Storybooks:
which combine scientific facts with fun underwater storylines
for ages 3-6

Book 1 - 'Logan the Lobster' - was published in June 2020
Logan was different from all the other little lobsters.
Would they be his friends?
Would they play with him?

Book 2 - 'Prickle the Puffer Fish' was published in November 2020
A coral reef can be a very dangerous place to live.
How can Prickle keep herself safe?
How can she stop feeling so scared?
Can she be brave?
Prickle, the tiny puffer fish, needs to find the answers to these very
important questions.

The stories for little people are entertaining, informative and a good introduction
to the myriad and diverse life in the oceans. These are tales which deal with a
wide variety of moral values, feelings and other aspects of personal and social
well-being. Great for parents to share with youngsters with lots of starting points
for discussion!

School Visits:

Gloria loves visiting schools as the _'WeirdFish Lady'_ –
an educational advisor using the natural world to
inspire and encourage young people to understand
their planet. Book a visit -
email: gloria@barnettauthor.co.uk

Footprint to the Future:

Footprint to the Future - a social enterprise producing teaching resources and fiction books for children and adults to help understanding of Planet Earth.

Available Now: –
'Ocean World Teacher's Resource'

WHY teach about the oceans?

Plastic pollution and climate change are big subjects at the moment and all children need to have information which informs them of the problems facing Planet Earth. Oceans play an important role in supplying oxygen for all life on the planet. While rain forests and land plants supply 20% of the earth's oxygen, plankton from the oceans supply 70% of oxygen and sea grass contributes 10% - making oceans the biggest producer of oxygen on our planet. Keeping our planet's oceans healthy means looking after plankton and sea grass and thus preserving the oxygen supply for all animals on Earth, including humans.

Fossil fuel use has meant that excess carbon dioxide has been released into the atmosphere, which is then absorbed by the oceans. This excess carbon dioxide in oceans turns to carbonic acid, so oceans are turning acidic. There has already been a decline in the numbers of plankton in the oceans due to this rise in acidity.

Pollution of the oceans is not only about plastic pollution, but also about acidity, sewage, and other problems for ocean life such as overfishing. The Ocean World Teacher's Resource can help students to understand the problems in the world's oceans - but also to learn about the sea creatures and understand their diverse world. By working through the ideas in this Teacher's Resource and sharing their understanding, students can be awarded an 'Ambassador of the Oceans' certificate.

This resource on Oceans educates children (age 8-12) in the ecosystem of oceans, to understand the creatures that live in the oceans, and the importance of stopping pollution and keeping oceans healthy. It's all part of the BIG picture of understanding how our planet works.

Footprint to the Future has put together a package which allows the teacher to become an overnight expert on the world's oceans. What they receive is a selection of flexible learning activities, Power Points, original film clips, a film guide and games.

Details are available at: www.footprinttothefuture.co.uk

Gloria is co-author of the 'Ocean World Teachers' Resource' (for ages 8-12) which is on sale now – go to the www.footprinttothefuture.co.uk website